CORRECTIONS IN EARLY QUR'ĀN MANUSCRIPTS

CORRECTIONS IN EARLY QUR'ĀN MANUSCRIPTS

TWENTY EXAMPLES

DANIEL ALAN BRUBAKER

Front cover: MS.474.2003, courtesy of the Museum of Islamic Art (D. Brubaker photograph); back cover: BnF *arabe* 331, Bibliothéque nationale de France

Photographs of manuscripts from the following institutions are used by permission:

- Bibliothéque nationale de France, Paris
- Museum of Islamic Art, Doha
- The National Library of Russia, St. Petersburg

Modern Qur'ān images are from the Muṣḥaf Muscat, used by permission of DecoType.

Corrections in Early Qur'ān Manuscripts: Twenty Examples, Quran Manuscript Change Studies (series) Vol. 1

ISBN13: 978-1-949123-03-6 (paperback)

ISBN13: 978-1-949123-04-3 (e-book)

For my parents

CONTENTS

Transliteration Key   xi
Manuscripts Referenced   xv
Preface   xvii
Acknowledgments   xxvii

1. Introduction   1
2. The Corrections   27
3. Conclusions   93

Index of Qurʾān verses referenced   103
Further Reading   105
Glossary   109
About the Author   113

TRANSLITERATION KEY

For Arabic transliteration, I use the IJMES system, shown below. However, since my purpose is to emphasize the form of script rather than its pronunciation, I don't change the definite article *lām* to the sound of the "sun" letters immediately following it.

ء ʾ

ب b

ت t

ث th

ج j

ح ḥ

خ kh

د d

ذ dh

ر r

ز z

س s

ش sh

ص ṣ

ض ḍ

ط ṭ

ظ ẓ

ع ʿ

غ gh

ف f

ق q

ك k

ل l

م m

ن n

ه h

و w

ي y

ة -a (-at in construct state)

ال al- and ʾl- (article)

ا or ى ā

و ū

ي ī

يّ iyy

وُ uww

وَ aw

يَ ay

َ a

ُ u

ِ i

When I need to transliterate the bare *rasm*, I use Thomas Milo's system of capital letters to convey the ambiguity of archigraphemes in manuscripts:

A	ا	ـا
B	ٮ	ـٮ
G	ح	ـح
D	د	ـد
R	ر	ـر
S	س	ـس
C	ص	ـص
T	ط	ـط
E	ع	ـع
F	ڡ	ـڡ
[F]-Q	ٯ	ـٯ
K	ك	ـك
L	ل	ـل
M	م	ـم
[B]-N	ں	ـں
H	ه	ـه
W	و	ـو
[B]-Y	ى	ـى

MANUSCRIPTS REFERENCED

Bibliothèque nationale de France, Paris
   arabe **327** (examples 7 and 9)
   arabe **328** (examples 2 and 12)
   arabe **330** (example 8)
   arabe **331** (example 10)
   arabe **340** (example 13)

Cairo Al-Hussein Mosque
   Cairo *muṣḥaf al-sharīf* (example 16 and "Another phenomenon" at the end of chapter 2)

Dar al-Makhtutat, Ṣanʿāʾ
   01-20.4 (example 3)

Museum of Islamic Art, Doha
   MIA.2013.19.2 (example 15)
   MIA.2014.491 (example 20)
   MS.67.2007.1 (example 6)

MS.474.2003 (example 5, and front cover)

National Library of Russia, St. Petersburg
    Marcel 2 (example 4)
    Marcel 5 (example 19)
    Marcel 7 (example 18)
    Marcel 11 (example 3 and 17)
    Marcel 13 (example 3)
    Marcel 21 (example 3)

Topkapı Palace Library, Istanbul
    Topkapı *muṣḥaf al-sharīf* (examples 1, 11, and 14)

PREFACE

Over the several years since defending my doctoral dissertation, "Intentional Changes in Qurʾān Manuscripts," I've received many inquiries about when this work will be published. The delay has been the result of several factors, foremost among them a personal tendency toward perfectionism that keeps me revising in what sometimes feels like an endless loop. Another is the sheer, and growing, volume of the material that I have accumulated.

The book in your hands is a small attempt in the short term to give some satisfaction to those eager for this work by providing a representative sample and introduction. It is unusual, I think, for the popular-level publication to precede the full academic one, and I have been cautioned by some against doing this. I feel this situation is a special case — and at any rate I am happy to release this material even as I finalize the larger and more rigorous works.

In the following pages, I've written to be understood not only by scholars but also by general readers, though without, I hope, compromise of academic integrity. It is not a big book, but it does include some technical details, as it should. If you are a non-specialist, there may be things that go over your head. Please do not worry about it too much. Conversely, if you are an academic, you may find yourself wishing for more detail. If this is the case for you, I do hope you will at least derive some benefit from what I have done here, but also wait patiently as I finalize further publications.

This book does not engage in theological analysis of the Qurʾān's content. Though theology is a thoroughly legitimate subject of study and serious contemplation, I do not comment in these pages upon the ultimate spiritual questions that the Qurʾān raises. This book is not the place for it. What I have done is introduce an aspect of textual criticism of the Qurʾān that has occupied my interest and effort and that I find fascinating.

Still, it may be appropriate to consider *why* the Qurʾān as an object is worthy of such attention, what difference it should make to most people that the book exists, and why regular folks might be curious about its early transmission history.

The first thing to note is that the Qurʾān's ideas and theology have not only had an impact on world history for more than a thousand years, but they continue to affect the lives of billions of people today. Those affected include people who believe Muhammad was a prophet and those who do not.

Let me address several potential categories of readers, one or more of which may represent you, and discuss what profit there may be in the subject of this book for each.

First, if you are one who believes Muhammad was a prophet and you call yourself "Muslim:" The Qur'ān is, quite simply, your *kitāb*, your book. Obviously, you know this. When it comes to these manuscripts, they are among the earliest surviving witnesses to the message Muhammad delivered. The verses they contain are likely those to which Muhammad was referring when he is reported to have said that Allah "showed favor to the believers when He sent among them an apostle from among themselves who recited to them His verses and purified them and taught them the book and wisdom, though before they were in obvious error."[1] For this reason alone I suggest it makes sense to have a curiosity about the early manuscripts. What passages do they contain? What are their physical and textual features? What variations exist among them, and what can these mean? What are these corrections, and why do they exist? And so forth. These manuscripts are fascinating to me as a scholar, and they capture my imagination every time I handle them or think about where and when they came into being. I can only imagine how special they must be to a person who believes they contain records of revelation.

Second, what might be the interest for those who do not believe Muhammad was a true prophet and therefore do not believe the Qur'ān to be revelation from God? To this I would answer that, even so, there are indeed some 1.6 billion people in this world who do believe that Muhammad was a prophet and who thus live their lives in some degree of conformity to his message and instructions. Depending upon where you live, you may have a lot of direct interaction with such people, or a little, or perhaps none at all. But the world is changing constantly and the influence of ideas upon events distant and local is all around us. It is probably not necessary for you (if you fall into this category) to engage deeply with the literary or devotional sources of the religion of Muhammad, but a reasonable level of information — some of it on the cutting edge of research — about the history and documentary trail of the foundational text of this world faith, the Qurʾān, is worth acquiring, if possible, and some of that is contained in the pages that follow here. Also, in my view, the main contours of the book you hold in your hands are not terribly difficult to grasp, even for non-Arabists. Give it a go!

Third, if you are an academic (either believing or non-believing), the purpose of your work is to uphold truth and to pursue knowledge. Yes, it is true that everyone has a reason and motivation that draws our interest to a particular subject — you do as well as I. But to be a good scholar, one must operate in methodologically sound ways, and in service of a common master: Truth. When it comes to the history of Muhammad's life and actions, to that of those who identified with him during that time and in the subsequent Arab conquests, to the history of the revelation and its transmission, and to the content of that revelation, the circumstances of its delivery, and the exegetical (interpretive) keys that may have been given by Muhammad and related through his companions and others, there is a lot to unpack and a lot more uncertainty about some details than most uncritical observers may understand. As scholars we intend to test claims and propositions, with the purpose of refining our understanding of what actually happened or (as the case may be) what was actually said or written. Today we are witnessing an exhilarating time, academically, for the study of Qurʾān manuscripts and their early history. As an academic who is presumably interested in this field (since you are reading this), you may be very encouraged.

Fourth, if you are a professional (either believing or non-believing) in politics or government or media, you may be faced from time to time, and perhaps increasingly, with claims about Islam, both positive and negative. Depending upon your personal relationships, predilections, political leanings, or any number of other factors, you may be inclined to believe one or the other. But in any given situation you might be wrong or lack nuance. When you speak, people listen to you. When you make a policy decision, it affects others. Good governance, reporting, and managing of others rests ideally upon knowledge and wisdom. Sometimes the critical or negative thing — even though not politically correct — might be true. At other times, the alarming generalization — even though satisfying to believe — might not be true or may at least require some qualification. The very center of Islam is Muhammad, and the center of Muhammad's identity for Muslims is his status as a Messenger of Allah. A messenger has a message, and the Qur'ān is that of Muhammad; therefore, its history is not an inconsequential matter.

This book, as I have already said, will not speak to the larger issues of Islam. But it does focus on tangible historical objects that, because of their particular characteristics as described here, do challenge traditional assertions about the transmission of the Qur'ān in several ways. If you are a curious and inquisitive person (and these are really good and important qualities in any human being, all the more so for those whose professions are related to knowledge, policy, and opinion), this book might be of interest to you not only for what it says about the matter at hand but also for what it says about what might be termed a pious enhancement of the Qur'ān's textual history. Hagiography, the enhancement of a history in order to elevate its subject, is not only carried out on historical people; it can be directed toward objects as well and — setting aside completely for the moment the entire matter of the *actual* nature of the Qur'ān as received by Muhammad himself — the history of this recitation as a physical object from the time of its writing down until the present appears to contain some elements of hagiography, or cleaning up and beautifying. To acknowledge this is not necessarily to suggest bad or nefarious motives and certainly it is quite natural for people to attribute the most complimentary attributes and circumstances to people or objects that they hold in great esteem. But if it is our intention to deal in reality, as is or ought to be the case for historians and reporters and legislators alike, we should be willing to test assumptions.

The past dozen years have been an adventure for me. I became interested in Qur'ān manuscripts while working on my PhD in the department of Religious Studies (now the department of Religion) at Rice University in Houston. In fact it was at a conference in Oxford around that time, perhaps 2007, that I first heard Keith Small present a paper on textual criticism of the Qur'ān. I had further conversations with Keith on the subject at that time, and he, in his characteristic kindness and humility, made himself available to mentor me as I became ever more interested over the next several years.

Keith invited me to deliver a paper as part of a panel at the annual meeting of the Middle East Studies Association

(MESA) in San Diego, organized by Emran El-Badawi and chaired by David Powers. I had been examining photographs of Qur'ān manuscripts (for example from the UNESCO CD-Rom of Sanʿāʾ Qur'ans) more closely, and found a very interesting page with two corrections and one glaring non-canonical variant that had not been corrected. I discussed these findings in my conference paper.

During a break between sessions at that conference, Keith and I were talking in the sitting area of his hotel room in the Grand Hyatt (it looked right out over the Bay and the day was sunny and beautiful) and Keith showed me a couple of photographs that really caught my attention: they were pictures of Qur'ān manuscript pages that had quite dramatic and lengthy corrections on them. These were not just a few letters or a single word, but were overwritten erasures greater than a full line in length. I found the photographs fascinating and surprising.

Already very interested, I decided to look more at the early development of the written Qur'ān in my doctoral work, thinking at first that I wanted to write my dissertation on something in the area of textual criticism related to these manuscripts generally, including corrections as part of the picture. As I began this project, I began to find more corrections, and I took note of them. In 2011 I made a major research trip to Europe and the Middle East to view manuscripts. Although my original idea for my dissertation was to write on early development of the Qur'ān in written form, I began to think seriously about writing only on corrections. I contacted Keith once again and asked his opinion of this direction. He said it would be a very good topic, so I told David Cook and my department of the new subject I intended to pursue.

The rest is now history. I successfully defended my dissertation and was awarded my doctorate from Rice in April 2014, and have been continuing my research in this area since. Whereas I had documented some 800 physical corrections in my dissertation, I have by now noted thousands, and there is no end in sight.

What do these corrections indicate? You will see my own brief remarks in the final chapter.

I am aware, of course, that my work deals with things that real people believe, feel in their hearts, and consider to be matters of cultural and personal honor, so it is appropriate that I speak about this aspect for a moment.

The matter of corrections in Qurʾān manuscripts obviously touches the question of whether what we have now is a true and complete representation of what was delivered by Muhammad in the first part of the 7th century AD.[2] This question is quite different from the (also important) one of whether Muhammad was a prophet — that is, whether these revelations are from God. The book you have in your hands, and the material contained within it, does not have anything to say about whether Muhammad was a prophet. It does have to do with questions about the Qurʾān's original form and about the integrity of its transmission in the earliest stages after Muhammad's death. I am not trying to hurt anyone's feelings by studying these things or by talking about them. What I would like to do, both as a human being and as a scholar, is test assumptions and follow evidence where it leads. I propose this path is a good one for anyone to follow, and so I invite you to come along this road as well.

As mentioned earlier, my more extensive works are forthcoming; I do hope those interested will wait patiently a little while longer and receive these warmly when they are soon, God willing, published.

At the back of this book is a list of further reading.

Daniel Alan Brubaker

May, 2019

---

1. Guillaume, A., *The Life of Muhammad: A translation of Ibn Isḥāq's* Sirāt Rasūl Allāh, (Oxford: Oxford University Press, 1955. 398). See also Qurʾān 3:164.
2. A note on dating conventions: I reference dates throughout this book in the Gregorian (solar) calendar, that is, "AD" and "BC." Many readers will be aware that there is also an Islamic lunar calendar that dates from the year in which Muhammad and his community emigrated from Mecca to Medina, 622 AD, an event called the *hijra*. Its dates are given in (lunar) years as "AH," for *anno hijrī*. In many scholarly books dealing with subjects related to Islam and its history, dates are given in both AD (or "CE") and AH. For simplicity and ease of reference to the calendar familiar to most readers, I have chosen not to do this in the English edition. If readers wish to find corresponding *hijrī* dates in a given instance, there exist today many free phone apps and online calculators that make doing so very easy.

ACKNOWLEDGMENTS

Many people have made my Qurʾān manuscript work to date possible and pleasant, but there are some in particular whom I would be remiss not to mention by name.

First, I am grateful to my Ph.D. advisor David Cook and the late Keith Small, both academic mentors to me, and both also dear friends. I am also grateful to have had the guidance and friendship of the late Andrew Rippin, and am particularly thankful for the honor of his presence on my doctoral committee.

Many owners, curators, caretakers, and staff of institutions housing the manuscripts have opened doors for me, and I am grateful to all, including the following: Olga Vasilyeva and the manuscript staff at the National Library of Russia; Sue Kaoukji, her team at the Dar Museum (Kuwait); Dr. Mounia Chekhab Abudaya, Marc Pelletreau, and the entire staff at the Museum of Islamic Art in Doha; Marie Geneviève Guesdon at the Bibliothèque nationale de France; Alasdair Watson and the staff of the Special Collections Reading Room at Oxford University; Catherine Ansorge and Yasmin Faghihi at the Cambridge University Library; Elaine Wright at the Chester Beatty Library (Dublin); Colin Baker for making available to me both the actual manuscript BL2165 as well as a personal copy of his facsimile edition of the same in September of 2013 at the British Library; Samar Al Gailani of the Beit Al Qurʾān as well as its curator, Ashraf Al Ansari; Dr. Halit Eren in Istanbul for his hospitality in 2011 and to IRCICA and Dr. Tayyar Altıkulaç (who I have yet to meet) for his wonderful work in preparing the Turkish facsimile editions of important Qurʾān *maṣāḥif*; ISAM; the Muslim Board of Uzbekistan for their assistance on my 2016 visit to Tashkent; and Amalia Zhukovskaya and Alla Sizova at the Institute of Oriental Manuscripts in St. Petersburg for their help during my several visits there.

Colleagues who have offered help and/or hospitality in this work include Efim Rezvan, Gerd-R and Elisabeth Puin (who hosted me as a houseguest and have invited me again), Alba Fedeli, and François Déroche.

I give a friendly nod also to colleagues at both the Islamic Manuscript Association (particularly Davidson MacLaren) and the International Qurʾanic Studies Association (particularly Emran El-Badawi).

Latha and I owe a personal debt to Joshua Lingel for his steady encouragement over many years. He is a dear friend.

In 2012, having become aware of his unique expertise and long work in the area of historically and scientifically sound Arabic typography and encoding, I began pursuing Thomas Milo to develop much-needed solutions specific to my own needs dealing with Qurʾān manuscripts, in particular related to the un-disambiguated *rasm*.[1] We had conversations around this topic over the following two years, and the conversation continues. I am heartened today to see fruit coming in large part through the clear outside-the-box thinking and aesthetic sense possessed by him and Mirjam, who have become friends to us. I am so grateful. They are kind, smart, and talented people.

I am grateful to my friend and colleague Roy Michael McCoy III (Ph.D. as of January 2019) who in this post-doctoral stage has assisted immensely with, among other things, transfer of my research from notes and photographs to the database I designed for the purpose of organizing and containing this material; it has been a privilege to work alongside him and my other colleague and friend, Andy Bannister - whose talents and energies seem to know no end.

The following people read and offered helpful peer-review comments on this book, in more than one instance saving me from a great deal of embarrassment. I owe each of them sincere thanks: Marijn van Putten, Gerd-R. Puin, Asma Hilali, and Mark Durie. Further, I thank Leah Garber for her thorough proofreading for grammar, punctuation, and style.

Finally, I thank my dear (also talented, accomplished, kind and beautiful) wife, Latha, for being my partner in life's work. I also thank my parents, Alan and Susan Brubaker, as well as hers, Annamma and the late Jefreys K. Samuel, for bringing us into the world, for raising us with much love and sacrifice, and in particular for helping during the long hours and days of my doctoral work and beyond.

Having said all this, the work that follows is my own and I take responsibility for shortcomings that persist. I hope it proves for all readers an enjoyable and informative introduction to a fascinating topic.

---

1. There is a glossary at the back of this book defining specialized terms, including this one. The *rasm*, as I use the term, is the basic shape of the Arabic consonantal text, without its dots or short vowels.

INTRODUCTION

Early Qur'ān manuscripts contain many physical changes or corrections.[1] By now I have taken note of thousands of such changes via careful examination of these manuscripts, mostly in person. This book is meant to serve as an overview, providing examples to illustrate the general nature of these manuscript corrections. In subsequent works I will make a more extensive presentation of these corrections and their descriptions.

ABOUT EARLY QUR'ĀN MANUSCRIPTS

A wealth of Qur'ān manuscript fragments have survived from the first several centuries of its life. Many of the important early manuscripts are now available to scholars like myself as a result of such political circumstances as Napoleon's campaign in Egypt and Syria which was accompanied by the deployment of scholars such as Jean-Joseph Marcel,[2] or as the result of the intrepid efforts of people like Jean-Louis Asselin de Cherville,[3] Agnes Smith Lewis and Margaret Dunlop Gibson,[4] Chester Beatty,[5] Edward Henry Palmer,[6] and others, who acquired and preserved these objects. There have indeed been many different people involved in the collection and safekeeping of these manuscripts and these are only a few of the important names behind the objects in western academic libraries today. There are more manuscripts safely (others, sadly, have been imperiled by wars and other political instabilities) kept in institutions around the world, and these all have stories and individuals behind them. It has taken me time and effort over a number of years to learn the locations of many such manuscripts, and I have had the privilege now of visiting a large number, including those probably produced in the 7th and 8th centuries AD, in libraries and museums around the world.

With some very important exceptions — most notably the Qur'āns that tradition tells us the third Caliph, 'Uthmān, burned and that would therefore be forever lost — we seem to have a good number of early Qur'ān manuscripts from a fairly early date. Why are there so many Qur'ān manuscripts in existence from the first and second centuries after Muhammad's life? In addition to the relative recency of this revelation[7] when compared to (for example) the biblical writings, there are two additional main reasons.

First, by the 7th century AD (Muhammad, the sources tell us, lived from 570 to 632), parchment was a commonly used material to receive writing, particularly for books.[8] Parchment is animal skin, and unlike papyrus which will typically disintegrate over a period of 100-200 years, documents written on parchment can endure for thousands of years. They do not always last this long as other factors, such as the acidity of the ink used for writing, the quality and thickness of the parchment itself, and the humidity and other environmental factors the document has endured, contribute to their lifespan. But in general, the relative stability of parchment has resulted in a very large number of Qur'ān manuscripts from these important early centuries having survived for us to examine.

A second major reason for the survival of so many Qur'ān manuscripts from the early period is the fact that, beginning in the mid-7th century AD (that is, the first century after Muhammad) these were produced in political environments that viewed the book in a positive light. The ruling authorities in these regions were not hostile to the Qur'ān as was the situation for the New Testament during the first two centuries of Christianity. It was not dangerous to own a copy of the Qur'ān in the Arab empires that by the latter part of the 7th century stretched across a huge swath of territory from the Iberian Peninsula and the Maghreb in the West to Azerbaijan in the East, nor were these manuscripts usually destroyed if discovered. In fact, to own such an object was a sign of status, wealth, and piety. These documents were finely produced and at great cost. Professional scribes were employed and good materials used, the best that could be afforded by the person who commissioned a copy. As time progressed, the production of Qur'āns became an art in itself with precise rules of geometry, ruling, and letter form. Illuminations were applied in various colors including gold leaf. These were treasured possessions that held a place of prominence and were displayed openly in mosques, palaces, and private residences.

HOW MANUSCRIPTS ARE DATED

The first question people tend to ask when looking at one of these manuscripts is, "How old is it?" Obviously, we want to know when a manuscript was produced, because its date allows us to (a) better understand what the object can tell us about its time, and (b) apply what we may already know about that period as a lens to help us understand what we see going on in the manuscript itself. So, the date is very important.

It would be nice if every manuscript came with a label stating when it was produced. In fact, it became customary in later Qurʾān manuscripts to include a colophon with such information as the name of the scribe and the date of production. Unfortunately, we do not have such neat and clean indications for manuscripts of the first several centuries.

These manuscripts, then, are dated by considering what information we do have, and this typically includes things such as *paleography*, or the study of the development of script styles. We have a good sense of when particular styles of script and certain developments in the ways of writing Arabic were in use, and so this detail of a manuscript is very important. The script style classifications that are standard today were described by François Déroche in the 1980s. In general, the script styles listed in rough chronology of their *first appearance* are: "hijazi" or "māʾil" (these two terms are used interchangeably), O, A & B.Ia (similar time of origin), C, B.II, D, E, F, and "New Style."[9] These styles do overlap; one was on the rise as another was still in use or in decline, for example, and even this statement only takes into account the chronological dimension; doubtless regional and economic factors play into the picture as well. Most of these styles have subcategories. It is not an exact science — for example, it is common for a manuscript to match Prof. Déroche' description of a style along most but not all of its defining features — but this should surprise no one when it is remembered that the scribes were human (scribes' personal styles are most readily observed in the earlier scripts) and that there was a progression over time and geography.

The earliest Qur'ān manuscripts, particularly those in the "hijazi" or "mā'il" styles, were written without diacritic marks or with only occasional diacritic marks to disambiguate the archigraphemes. This is not to say, however, that the only way to disambiguate the archigraphemes was via diacritics. In fact, there came to be a system of writing the Arabic *rasm* that allowed precise disambiguation without those extraneous marks, and Thomas Milo has termed this system "script grammar."[10]

A second helpful indication can be the features of the page or book beyond the writing itself. The study of these features is called *codicology*.[11] Codicology asks questions like these: What is the writing material? Is the page vertical or horizontal in format? What are the dimensions of the page or book? How many lines of writing are on each page? Do all pages have the same number of lines, or does the number vary? How are the verses and chapters divided, and what sort of marks are used to do so? What inks were used? Is the page illuminated with illustrations or other graphic elements, including extra markings to represent the short vowels? If so, what colors were used and what forms or styles or particular types of elements are present? Are the lines of the pages ruled? Are the margins ruled? Do margins exist or does the writing extend to the edge of the page? How is (or was) the book sewn together? What sort of binding was used? These features and more can provide details that give additional clues as to the age of a manuscript.

A third method for dating is probably the most well-known: radiocarbon dating. This method can be applied to anything organic. Everything that was once living, that is, all plant or animal material, is organic. Parchment qualifies, and can therefore be tested with this method. The reason radiocarbon dating works is that a radioactive isotope of carbon is present in all living things and begins to slowly decay at a predictable rate when the living thing dies. Subjecting parchment to this testing yields a series of date ranges based upon the probable time that the source (in this case most likely the goat or sheep) was alive.

Obviously a radiocarbon date range cannot tell when a parchment was written, but we generally assume that a parchment did not sit for decades before receiving its first writing.

Radiocarbon dating is not a foolproof way of determining dates of manuscripts. Some manuscripts of known date of origin (e.g. with a colophon or some other overt indication of the time of writing) have been radiocarbon dated a century or more off from the apparent actual date of production. Therefore, all these methods must be taken with a grain of salt, and in most cases the best thing is to take all the various clues (paleography, codicology, and radiocarbon dating if available), and weigh them alongside one another.[12]

PROVENANCE

In dealing with any ancient artifact, we want to consider all available information about it. At first view, we may be tempted to imagine that we can discern everything important about a manuscript merely from its physical details — what it says, what it does not say, how it was written, how it was ornamented, the material upon which it was written and the ink(s) that were used, how it was bound, whether the page was ruled, and so forth.

However, an object's *context* can also be very important to historians. There is always a context in which an item was produced, and there were contexts through which these objects have passed all the way until the time of their discovery (or re-discovery) and even after their discovery. Unfortunately, we cannot time-travel back to the moment and place of production, so it is very helpful to know at least where an item was found, by whom, and the chain of custody since that time. Where a manuscript was found may give further indication about where it was produced, during what time period, and by whom, as well as to how it was used post-production. Most of the manuscripts discussed in this book were not recently found on archeological digs, but were rather discovered in mosques or libraries or private family collections passed down through generations and at some point (for example) making their way into the stall of a flea market or antiquities dealer and then sold to a discerning buyer. Still, chain of custody is important for several reasons, including the authentication of an object in a world where the value of such items leads sometimes to forgeries. We certainly don't want to base our historical research about the past upon objects that are not authentic.

I don't go deeply into provenance in this book, but will say that much of the modern history of manuscripts shown is documented, and that institutions will often express caution about objects whose provenance has not been confirmed or is doubtful. Furthermore, once an image such as a photograph is made of an object, that image also becomes an object. Who took the picture, where, and when? Citing the photographer, whether he or she is a museum staff member or a researcher like myself who was permitted access, should always be done when this information is available. This is both to give credit where due and also to describe the context of the object with due diligence.

It is important, finally, to understand that doubtful provenance does not mean that an object isn't authentic or that it should not be taken seriously. Nor does the existence of a solid chain of custody always mean that an ancient object must be authentic, though it does strengthen the case. Attention to provenance is merely one of the best practices in archeology that helps us do quality work and avoid making unnecessary errors.

CONSONANTAL VARIANTS

Leaving aside for a moment the matter of corrections to the page, there is variation in the consonantal text (in Arabic this is called the *rasm*) within early Qur'ān manuscripts. The traditional way of accounting for this variation is to claim that it was a flexibility approved by Muhammad himself and represented in variant readings, called *qirā'āt*. In fact, the readings are different from the *rasm* and in most cases the one is not affected in the least by the other. Indeed, the history of the codification or (if you will) canonization of these readings is more complex and, according to the recent work of Shady Nasser,[13] owed less to a historical root validating each of the particular readings than it did to pragmatic or practical and political concerns. In short, Nasser argues, the readings were chosen to give geographic representation during Ibn Mujāhid's time (late 9th and early 10th century AD) in the various urban centers from which he chose them, and not necessarily on the basis of strongest multiple attestation as is commonly supposed.

A further matter of difficulty for the readings is that the consonantal texts of some of the important monumental early codices, such as the Topkapı, Istanbul, and Cairo *maṣāḥif*, do not reflect a single reading, but rather what might appear to be a combination of the different readings.[14] This fact leads the preparer of their facsimile editions, Dr. Tayyar Altıkulaç, to describe these codices in terms of rough percentages when it comes to their adherence to the various readings. Such a circumstance is not necessarily irreconcilable with the existence of approved readings, but it does indicate a more complex picture that requires further inquiry and explanation.

That being said, many of the thousands of corrections I have documented appear to have nothing to do with the readings attested in the secondary literatures. So, corrections must represent in at least some cases another phenomenon, such as perhaps a greater degree of perceived flexibility of the Qur'ān text in its early centuries (the time of first production of these manuscripts) than is documented in the *qirā'āt* literature.

GENERAL OBSERVATIONS ABOUT CORRECTIONS

You will see details of corrections in the next chapter, but will not get a full sense of the relative prevalence of different types of correction or their other features, so here is a high-level view. In a correction, something is added (insertion), removed (erasure), replaced (erasure overwritten, taping overwritten, or overwriting without erasure), or (perhaps) hidden. Corrections can be classified in other ways but these terms summarize the mechanics of the matter. I discuss the last category briefly at the end of the next chapter.

Most of the time, I have found that corrections in a Qurʾān manuscript result in conformity of that manuscript at the point of the correction with the *rasm* of the now-standard 1924 Cairo edition. This pattern is important and shows a general movement over time toward conformity, though not immediate complete conformity. There are interesting questions raised when a manuscript is corrected in one place but remains deviant (the word "deviant" supposes a standard and I use it here merely as a practical matter) when compared to the 1924 Cairo edition in other places. We will discuss this scenario more later.

Sometimes a correction takes a manuscript away from conformity with the now-standard *rasm*. The first thing to consider when that is observed is whether the correction has followed a regional variant, and for this possibility there is a secondary literature to consult. Very rarely, a correction actually takes the manuscript out of conformity with any documented variant or reading, so such instances are interesting when they are found.

Because each correction is different in nature and significance, it would be a mistake to draw conclusions from raw numbers, but for general information, here is a rough breakdown of the relative number of instances so far.[15]

- Erasure overwritten — about 30%

- Insertion — about 24%
- Overwriting without erasure — about 18%
- Simple erasure — about 10%
- Covering overwritten — about 2%
- Covering — about 16%

More important factors to consider than the mechanics of a change include the apparent reason(s) for it, its timing relative to that of the first production of the manuscript, its extent, and what has been altered. Relevant questions about these matters, and more, will be discussed at the end of this introduction.

WHERE ARE THESE MANUSCRIPTS TODAY?

Because of factors such as the climate of the region of their production and the material upon which they were generally written (parchment), a very large number of early Qurʾān manuscripts have survived the centuries and exist in private and public collections. My own work over the past dozen years has been an exciting process of discovery of (among many other things) where they are. I now have a very long list and in my travels have noted collections both large and small. Undoubtedly, there are many of which I have yet to become aware — including those in private collections.

But in terms of a general understanding, which is the point of this book, these manuscripts exist in various university and national libraries, such as Cambridge, Oxford, the University of Birmingham, the John Rylands Library in Manchester, and Berlin, as well as in museums around the world such as the Museum of Islamic Art in Doha, the Tareq Rajab Museum and the Dar Museum in Kuwait, the British Library in London, the Chester Beatty Library in Dublin, and the Beit al-Qurʾān in Manama, and the Biruni Institute or Oriental Studies in Tashkent, to name a few. Thanks is also owed to private donors and collectors, such as Nasser D. Khalili, who have gathered and safeguarded these objects and who make them available to scholars for study.

HISTORY OF THE QURʾĀN (TRADITIONAL)

What is commonly accepted about the early history of the Qurʾān has reached us mainly through secondary literatures that were written down beginning in the closing decades of the 8th century (that is, about 150-160 years after the death of Muhammad). These literatures, though further removed in time from the events they describe than we might hope, are not without merit: but different scholars and historians have approached them in different ways. I will discuss this matter more later; the first thing is to relate a general outline of the traditional account, that is, what most Muslims and most casual observers accept as "what happened." Here it is:

Muhammad was born in 570 AD, in Mecca. His father died before the time of his birth and his mother died when Muhammad was yet very young. Henceforward, Muhammad was raised by his grandfather and then by his uncle. As a young adult, Muhammad entered the employ of a Meccan businesswoman named Khadija, who was significantly his senior. When he was 25, she proposed marriage and he accepted.

At age 40, Muhammad was spending time alone in a cave in the hills outside of Mecca where he sometimes went for quiet. Suddenly, he was encountered by an imposing being that seemed to cover the sky. It grabbed him tightly and gave the command *"iqra'!"* ("recite"), to which he answered, "What shall I recite?" Three times this happened, each time the being grabbing him even tighter. After the third time, tradition tells us, the first revelations — part of what is now the Qur'ān — began coming from his mouth.

Muhammad returned home in a sweat, not sure what had just happened. It was his wife, Khadija, who informed him that this had been the angel Gabriel and that Muhammad was a Messenger of God.

This first encounter was in 610 AD. Over the next 22 years (23 or so by the lunar calendar), Muhammad would continue to receive revelations from time to time. Sometimes they were long and sometimes short. Sometimes they were at close intervals and at other times long periods elapsed between revelations. When Muhammad would get a revelation, he ordinarily would begin reciting it publicly, for example in his prayers. Others among those who had become believers would listen, memorize, and recite as well, thus recording and transmitting the revelations orally. There are also hadith traditions that say Muhammad would have his personal secretary, Zayd b. Thabit, write down the revelations whenever he received them.

By the time of Muhammad's death in 632 AD, the revelations had been, we are told, written down on various discrete objects like palm stalks, stones, and bones of animals. These were gathered together, compiled and organized around this time, and written as a book (Arabic *muṣḥaf*).

Over the next couple of decades, later sources state, there came to be disagreements over some parts of the Qur'ān's content that were significant enough to require the resolution of the matter via production of authoritative copies and the destruction of those deemed variant. This process, we are told, was undertaken by the third Caliph, ʿUthman, who died in 656 AD. He commissioned the production of several authoritative copies and had these sent out to the main centers of the now large Arab empire that he oversaw.

ʿUthman's suppression of variants is not the end of the story, of course, even for the time period of the manuscripts which are considered in this book. These manuscripts go up through the 9th or possibly 10th centuries. We don't need to cover all that history here, but I should mention some major developments. By the closing years of the 7th century, the Arabs had conquered territory all the way from Azerbaijan in the East to the center of the Iberian Peninsula (via North Africa) in the West. By "conquered," we mean they had gained political control over the regions, not that they had settled or saturated the countryside or territories. The religion of Muhammad filtered out more gradually and organically into these areas over the subsequent decades and centuries.

There were rivalries and dynastic changes that occurred both regionally and across time. We don't need to cover all of these here either; some highlights include the start of the Umayyad dynasty of caliphs with the death of ʿAli, the fourth caliph who was also the cousin and son-in-law of Muhammad, in 661 AD. The Umayyads held authority over most of the Arab kingdom until the Abassid revolution in 750 A.D., and the Abassids, though shifting capitals (Baghdad, Kufa, Samarra, etc.) held sway until the mid-13th century.

DIFFICULT ISSUES

Some aspects of the Qur'ān, and some aspects of the historical records of the larger context of its transmission, including the details of the people and events in the first century of Islam, are a puzzle to historians. For the most part the Qur'ān's language is not complicated. However, it contains words and phrasings that seem to have been inscrutable even to believing exegetes going back to the early centuries of its history. Among these are words at whose meaning even the early commentators have had to guess.

For a book claiming to be revelation from God to contain mysteries, of course, would not itself be surprising. Some people, however, have raised the question of how such a circumstance can be reconciled to the Qur'ān's internal claim to have been "revealed in a clear (*mubīn*) Arabic tongue." (Q16:103)[16]

Devin Stewart, in considering words that break the rhyme structure of a passage, has entertained the possibility that the *rasm* at some time came to be mis-pointed in places by a later generation who did not have the benefit of an unbroken and complete oral tradition.[17] Such a theory, if true, would alter traditional assumptions about the Qur'ān's transmission history. In any event, extensive re-visiting of the received pointing of the Qur'ān text, that is, major revisionism, is probably not warranted. Still, I think it is entirely appropriate to consider the text in the way Devin has, and the rhyme words would just be markers that highlight a larger phenomenon. If it has happened with words that should rhyme, it would be unreasonable to think that it did not happen elsewhere as well — and the logical next thing to consider would be words that today pose difficulty for exegetes or that seem to be out of place. Could the *rasm* be read in a way that makes sense but is outside the received tradition of reading? The question has been considered.[18]

Following are a few more examples that highlight interesting questions and issues that critical scholars have been trying to address in recent years:

1) The **topography and other features of Mecca** does not seem to match descriptions in the Qurʾān. The Qurʾān itself is not rich in narrative detail, but this does not mean descriptions are lacking entirely. When one looks closely, there are solid things that may be observed. For example, the late Patricia Crone noticed the agricultural details in Q36 mention grain, date palms, and grapes, as well as gushing springs, with some echoes of these agricultural references appearing also in Q56. These descriptions are tied to the local pagans whom Muhammad was being instructed by Allah to warn. She notes many other agricultural references, most of which seem quite disconnected from the reality of Mecca.[19]

2) The **archaeology of Mecca** does not seem to support the traditional assertions that the place where Muhammad grew up and received the revelations was a location that had seen the rise and fall of many previous civilizations.

3) The **linguistic features** of the Qurʾān, in the opinion of some linguists[20] but not that of others,[21] raise questions about its place of origin. These are not, perhaps, questions irreconcilable at this point with the broad outlines of the traditional narrative, but neither are they insignificant.

4) The *qibla,* or direction of prayer, is designated by the orientation of the wall of the mosque containing its *miḥrāb,* the niche in the wall designating this direction. One recent

researcher, Dan Gibson, has noted that the surviving founda-
tions of all the earliest mosques until about 706 AD do not
point toward Mecca at all, but rather considerably further
north,[22] and such does indeed seem to be the case. After 706,
he finds *qibla*s began pointing in a direction further south
from the original direction but still north of Mecca, and the
first *qibla* he found pointing toward Mecca dates to around 727
AD. In fact, some process of development of the direction of
prayer is attested in the literatures of the time, with some indications that the direction was at first merely toward the east,[23]
though these sources diverge from others that indicate
Muhammad designating the *qibla* first toward Jerusalem and
then toward Mecca at a specific moment during his lifetime.[24]
Time will tell where scholarship lands on this matter as more
attention is directed toward reconciling the archaeology with
the contemporary historical literatures and other sources.

The apparent difference between what the Biography of
Muhammad (written by Ibn Isḥāq and revised by Ibn Hishām)
says on this matter and what is seen in the mosque founda-
tions highlights a larger and quite well-known issue that will
be mentioned again later: the reliability of the existing
secondary literatures, such as histories, *ḥadīth* collections,
biographical reports, and so forth. There is an extensive literature in Arabic from the 8th and 9th centuries relating history
of the previous century, but the documents contain internal
disagreements, sometimes without a clear clue for determining which side (if any) of a conflicting account is true. It is
not unusual to find equally "reliable" reports that are contra-
dictory.[25]

5) The **manuscripts** support some aspects of the traditional narrative, such as the approximate time period during

which quranic materials came to be written (for example, we have portions of Qurʾān manuscripts that appear to date from the mid-7th century), and they often confirm the existence of many of the various readings that are attested in the secondary literatures of the following century, but other features present a puzzle and need some sorting out.

First, many manuscripts do not follow a single reading but rather appear — to a person who is operating from the point of view of the documented canonical readings — to move between readings without a discernible pattern. This is not a problem but rather emphasizes the question, "What was the place of the readings at the time of production of these manuscripts?"

Second, there exist entire pages of parchment that have been washed or otherwise cleared of quranic material and then rewritten. These sheets, called *palimpsests*, are the most extensive corrections that have reached us. The wonderful thing about these documents is that in many cases what was first written on these pages can be discerned, either with the naked eye or through the use of technology that picks up the earlier text. I have not emphasized these in my research since others like Alba Fedeli, Elisabeth Puin, Asma Hilali, Éléonore Cellard, Behnam Sadeghi, and Mohsen Goudarzi have been working with them, but I will reference these as appropriate in later works.

Third, given the monumental nature of what tradition reports the third caliph, ʿUthmān, to have done with the standardization of the text — the suppression of variants via burning or other means of destruction, and the production of authoritative copies that were then to serve as exemplars and standards against which subsequent copies could be measured

— it is odd that no copy existing today has been reliably identified as one of these actual authoritative copies, and that the ones about which such a claim is made seem to have been produced long after ʿUthmān's time. Certainly there is evidence in the lower text of the aforementioned palimpsests that there were earlier forms of the text, but this does not solve the problem of the apparent lack of any of ʿUthmān's copies existing today. These documents would have been extremely important objects, so we would expect they would have been preserved.

Fourth, the existence of manuscripts that were finely produced yet sometimes corrected after a long passage of time is interesting and presents a challenge to the notion that there was a strict uniformity and widespread agreement about every detail, every word and letter, such as one would expect to find if there were widespread agreement upon a standard from a very early date, such as the time of ʿUthmān's caliphate. I will discuss some of my thoughts about this matter in "Conclusions."

WHY WERE CHANGES MADE?

Not all manuscript corrections are equal; each has a context and a situation involving time, place, writing materials, environment, exemplar, scholar, scribe, and so forth.

The most obvious cause that any one of us can easily imagine if we put ourselves in the place of working as a scribe is making a simple mistake when copying or writing, realizing the mistake, and then correcting it soon after.

A simple mistake-and-correction scenario fits what we see in some Qur'ān manuscript corrections where the ink, nib, and writing style appear to match that of the rest of the page. However, it does not fit all of them. In many cases there are clearly other factors at play. Here are some of the questions I ask that help me think carefully about what is going on in a given situation:

- Is there a discernible reason that could have caused a simple mistake? One of the common reasons for mistakes in manuscript transcription from an exemplar, for example, is the repeated occurrence of a word or sequence of words in close proximity to each other. A scribe may finish copying the first instance of the word or word sequence, go to dip the nib into the ink, and accidentally begin writing again after the second occurrence of the word or word sequence. This could be noticed later and corrected. Such a scenario or others like it is not uncommon in manuscript transmission.
- Was there a long passage of time between first writing and the moment(s) of correction? *This question can be pursued further by asking some of the following:*

1. Does it look as though the writing materials (ink and nib width, for example) used in the correction were similar to those used for the first production?
2. Is the writing style different from that of the main page? Is it a later script style, one that became popular in another time period? Is it of a different dimension (e.g., taller or shorter), or is it of a

different nib angle, or is it written by a person of a different writing or skill level?

3. Is there a difference of orthography (that is, the spelling or writing conventions that we know developed over time) between the page as first written and the part that has been corrected? Is the correction itself possibly dealing with such an issue?

Here are some further questions to consider:

- Does the page show signs of having been corrected more than once, at different times?
- What did the correction do? Can we see or guess what was first written?
- What was the result of the correction? Is the corrected *rasm* in harmony with the *rasm* of the standard text today? If it is not, and if the nature of the variant can be attributed to different orthographic norms, does its orthography align with other manuscripts from the time period? If it does not, or if the difference cannot be attributed to variant orthography, does it align with any of the variant readings acknowledged in the *qirāʾāt* literature?
- If the page has been corrected, what does the rest of the page look like? Are there other parts of the page that remain out of conformity with the now-standard *rasm*, and if so, what could this mean about the time that this document was corrected or about the person who corrected it?

Obviously, there are other questions one could ask, but you can, I hope, begin to see the way that we try to unpack these materials and make sense of them. You will see these questions in action as we turn now to the main substance of this book, and you can also ask them yourself as you look at each example.

---

1. I use the term "correction" for convenience, but I ask readers to please notice that the word itself carries a value judgment that I don't necessarily intend in each case. Was that which was first written necessarily less "correct"? Is what now stands always and necessarily more "correct"? Most of the time, the changes we find in Qur'ān manuscripts result in something that looks more or less like the *rasm* of the standard 1924 Cairo text, but there are exceptions. So, please bear in mind that when I use the term "correction," I intend only to mean a physical change to the script at some point.

2. Déroche, François, *Qur'ans of the Umayyads: A first overview,* (Leiden: Brill, 2014), 17.

3. Ibid.

4. Ansorge, Catherine, "Cambridge University Library Islamic Manuscript Collection. Origins and Content," *Journal of Islamic Manuscripts* 7 (2016): 139-40; Soskice, Janet, *The Sisters of Sinai: How Two Lady Adventurers Discovered the Hidden Gospels,* (New York: Alfred A. Knopf, 2009). The latter tells the fascinating story of how these two Scottish women traveled to North Africa and procured important biblical and quranic manuscripts that are today preserved in places like the Cambridge University Library.

5. A. Chester Beatty was a successful American businessman who used his wealth for many charitable endeavors, among which was the acquisition of manuscripts and other historic objects. Among the treasures he collected were some of the oldest papyrus fragments of the New Testament, and many Qur'ān fragments and complete manuscripts, some quite early. Most of his collection today is housed in the Chester Beatty Library, located in the Dublin Castle.

6. Ansorge, Catherine, "Cambridge University Library Islamic Manuscript Collection. Origins and Content," *Journal of Islamic Manuscripts* 7 (2016): 135.

7. I do not intend by this comparison to suggest that the Qur'ān belongs in the same category, *qua* revelation, as the Hebrew Bible and New Testament. I merely raise it in order to point out similarities and differences in the

context and circumstances that may have factored into the outworking of the various transmission histories.

8. Papyrus was indeed also in use extensively during this time period. Because of its lower cost, it was the writing material of choice for many administrative and transactional documents, as well as regular correspondence. Indeed, there are also examples of Qur'ān manuscripts written on papyrus. The few that I have seen (there are a couple in Oxford's Bodleian Library, for example) are small fragments. To my understanding, there are a fair number of Qur'ān manuscripts on papyrus, but I have not yet had the opportunity to understand their number or quality. The point here is that parchment use was widespread, and it is, at least in part, due to this fact that we today have so many well-preserved pages of early Qur'āns.

9. Déroche, François, *The Abbasid Tradition: Qur'ans of the 8th to the 10th centuries AD,* (London: Nour Foundation, 1992); Déroche, François, *Qur'ans of the Umayyads: A first overview,* (Leiden: Brill, 2014).

10. Milo, Thomas, "Towards Arabic historical script grammar through contrastive analysis of Qur'ān manuscripts," in *Writings and Writing: Investigations in Islamic Text and Script in honour of Januarius Justus Witkam.* Kerr, Robert and Thomas Milo, eds. (Cambridge: Archetype, 2013), 249-92.

11. Déroche, François, *Islamic Codicology: an introduction to the study of manuscripts in Arabic script,* (London: Al-Furqān Islamic Heritage Foundation, 2006).

12. Dutton, Yasin, "An Umayyad Fragment of the Qur'an and its Dating," in *Journal of Qur'anic Studies* 9, no. 2 (2007): 57-87.

13. Nasser, Shady, *The Transmission of the Variant Readings of the Qur'an: The Problem of Tawātur and the Emergence of Shawādhdh,* (Leiden: Brill, 2012).

14. What appears to be a combination of other attested readings, of course, may be simply its own reading.

15. These rough figures are mostly from my own work but also take into account some corrections in several manuscripts found by my friend and former research assistant, Dr. Roy Michael McCoy III. There is a great deal of additional material in my own notes and photographs not yet included in these numbers, and no doubt others will add to this body of research in the future, but at this point I do not expect a major shift in the relative proportions.

16. Ibn Kathīr, Ismāʿīl, *Tafsīr al-qur'ān al-ʿaẓīm,* (Beirut: Dar el-Marefah, 2003), 894-5. The commentaries (of which Ibn Kathīr is but one that is somewhat of a culmination taking into account the earlier historical and exegetical sources) place this verse in the context of accusations against Muhammad that he had been taught the Qur'ān by someone else, in particular a foreign servant who spoke only a little Arabic. This verse, then, is seen by

the commentators as an answer in which is implicit a rhetorical question: "How could a foreigner be the source of verses composed in pure Arabic?"

17. Stewart, Devin J., "Divine Epithets and the *Dibacchius: Clausulae* and Qur'anic Rhythm," *Journal of Qur'anic Studies* 15.2 (2013): 22-64. For further discussion of rhyme as an organizing feature, see Sinai, Nicolai, *The Qur'an: A historical-critical introduction,* (Edinburgh: Edinburgh University Press, 2017), 16-20.

18. Luxenberg, Christoph, *The Syro-Aramaic reading of the Koran: A contribution to the decoding of the language of the Koran,* (Berlin: Verlag Hans Schiler, 2007); Bellamy, James A., "Some Proposed Emendations to the Text of the Koran," *Journal of the American Oriental Society* 113, no, 4 (1993); Bellamy, James A., "More Proposed Emendations to the Text of the Koran," *Journal of the American Oriental Society* 116, no. 2 (1996).

19. Crone, Patricia, "How did the quranic pagans make a living?" *Bulletin of SOAS* 68, no. 3 (2005): 387-399.

20. Durie, Mark, *The Qur'an and its biblical reflexes: Investigations into the genesis of a religion,* (Lanham: Lexington Books, 2018), 16-17, 42-43 (note 22).

21. Nicolai Sinai (ibid., 42-43); van Putten, Marijn, "Hamzah in the Quranic Consonantal Text," in *Orientalia* 87 no. 1 (2018): 93-120.

22. Gibson, Dan, *Qur'ānic Geography: A survey and evaluation of the geographical references in the Qur'ān with suggested solutions for various problems and issues* (Altona: Independent Scholars Press, 2011).

23. Sharon, Moshe, "Qibla Musharriqa and early Muslim prayer in churches," in *The Muslim World* Vol. LXXXI, Nos. 3-4 (1991).

24. "And when the *qibla* was changed from Syria to the Ka'ba — it was changed in Rajab at the beginning of the seventeenth month after the apostle's arrival in Medina — Rifā'a b. Qays; Qardam b. 'Amr; Ka'b b. al-Ashraf; Rāfi' b. Abū Rāfi'; al-Hajjāj b. 'Amr, an ally of Ka'b's; al-Rabī b. al-Rabī' b. Abū'l-Ḥuqayq; and Kināna b. al-Rabī' b. Abū'l-Ḥuqayq came to the apostle asking why he had turned his back on the *qibla* he used to face when he alleged that he followed the religion of Abraham. If he would return to the *qibla* in Jerusalem they would follow him and declare him to be true. Their sole intention was to seduce him from his religion, so God sent down concerning them: 'The foolish people will say: What made them turn their back on the *qibla* that they formerly observed? Say, To God belongs the east and the west. He guides whom He will to the straight path. Thus we have made you a central community that you may be witnesses against men and that the apostle may be a witness against you. And we appointed the *qibla* which thou didst formerly observe only that we might know who will follow the apostle from him who turns upon his heels,' i.e. to test and find them out. 'Truly it was a hard test except for those whom God guided,' i.e. a temptation, i.e. those whom Allah established. 'It was

not Allah's purpose to make your faith vain,' i.e. your faith in the first *qibla*, your believing your prophet, and your following him to the later *qibla* and your obeying your prophet therein, i.e. so that he may give you the reward of both of them. 'God is kind and compassionate to men.'" Guillaume, A., *The Life of Muhammad: A translation of Ibn Isḥāq's* Sirāt Rasūl Allāh, (Oxford: Oxford University Press, 1955), 258-9.

25. One example is what the historian al-Ṭabarī relates about Muhammad's answer to the question about whether it was Isaac or Ishmael that Abraham took up the mountain to sacrifice. Half the accounts say that Muhammad answered, "Isaac," and half say that he answered "Ishmael." Brinner, William M., tr., *The History of al-Ṭabarī, volume II: Prophets and Patriarchs* (Albany: State University of New York Press, 1987), 82-97.

2
THE CORRECTIONS

I've chosen the following examples for this introduction to the range of the phenomenon. I could easily have chosen twenty others, and in subsequent installments may do so. Included below are corrections of various types (erasures, erasures overwritten, overwriting without erasure, and insertion) as well as of different script styles representing different early time periods (7th, 8th, and 9th centuries A.D.).

Since I understand that many readers of this book do not speak or read Arabic, I've made an effort to explain each change clearly in a way that will not be inscrutable to nonspecialists. Translation and graphic elements should serve this purpose while also including sufficient technical detail to satisfy those who want it. There will still be difficult elements for non-Arabic speakers, but I trust that the main point will be understood from the photographs and the accompanying descriptions.

Example 1: Post-production insertion of a word in a monumental 8th century Qur'ān

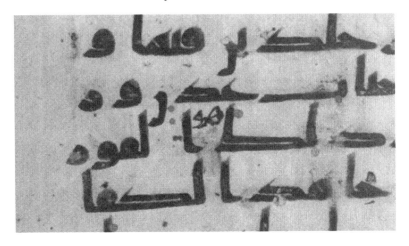

FIGURE I: *Topkapı* muṣḥaf al-sharīf, *fol. 122v. (Source: Altıkulaç, Tayyar,*
Ed. Al-Muṣḥaf al-Sharif attributed to ʿUthmān bin ʿAffān (The copy at
the Topkapı Palace Museum). Istanbul: IRCICA, 2007.)

This insertion is in the Topkapı codex commonly known as the Topkapı *muṣḥaf al-sharīf.* This codex, of 408 folios on vellum, is distinguished as one of the oldest complete (two folios are missing and others appear to have been replaced at an early date) copies of the Qur'ān. It was sent to Sultan Mahmud II in 1811 as a gift by M. Ali Pasha, then Governor of Egypt, and has been kept at the Topkapı Palace Museum since its arrival there in 1811.[1]

The Topkapı codex has been attributed by tradition to the third Caliph, ʿUthman, a Companion of Muhammad who died in 656 AD, about 24 years after Muhammad himself died. As is often the case with popular opinion, the attribution is not correct; this codex probably dates to a century later, that is, the mid-8th century AD. It is a delicate matter to challenge the attribution to 'Uthmān, so the statement of Mr. İhsanoğlu, the founding Director General of IRCICA and Secretary General of the Organisation of the Islamic Conference, is admirable and carries weight:

> Judging from its illumination, the Topkapı Museum *Muṣḥaf* dates neither from the period when the *Muṣḥaf*s of the Caliph 'Uthmān were written nor from the time when copies based on these *Muṣḥaf*s were written. Since *Muṣḥaf*s of the early period took those attributed to the Caliph 'Uthmān as a model, they do not have elements of illumination. [...] This *Muṣḥaf* [...] does not constitute a sample of the early period of *Muṣḥaf* writing due to a number of characteristics [...It] most probably belongs to the Umayyad period.[2]

The Topkapı codex is an important and beautifully-produced relatively early and nearly complete monumental Qur'ān manuscript. I hope to discuss it further in subsequent works.

I have noted 25 instances of correction over the Topkapı *muṣḥaf al-sharīf's* 408 folios. This, as well as examples 11 and 14, are representative. The photograph above shows an insertion of the word هو *huwa*, "it [is]," of Q9:72. In the 1924 Qur'ān, the affected phrase of this verse reads *wa-riḍwānun mina llāhi akbaru dhālika huwa 'l-fawzu 'l-ʿaẓīmu* "and Allah's good pleasure is greater, **that is** the great triumph."

The words *dhālika huwa* together mean "that is," but *dhālika* alone, which was part of the page as first written, carries the same basic meaning. In other words, this particular correction resulted in a manuscript that it is now in conformity with the now-standard *rasm,* but had no notable semantic effect.

This is clearly a post-production correction. It has been made with a different hand, nib, and style. It is my opinion that there was the passage of some length of time between production and correction.

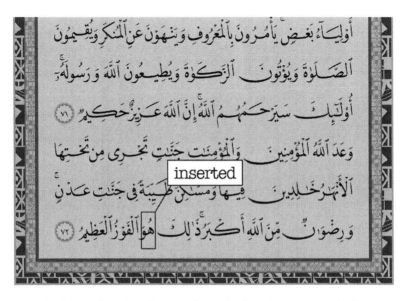

FIGURE 2: Illustration of location of correction Example 1 compared with the Azhar-approved mushafmuscat.com *Qurʾān, which is based upon the 1952 Cairo edition. [The 1952 edition corrected some errors in the 1924 Cairo edition. The mushafmuscat is basically the corrected 1924 edition with Omani-style punctuation. Also, the mushafmuscat follows the Medina format of 604 pages with a verse number at the end of each page for the entire Qurʾān, in contrast to the Cairo edition's free flowing text over 827 pages. The rasm is the same between these editions except for the position of some of the amphibious characters. On the 1924 and 1952 editions, see Puin, Gerd-R, "Quellen, Orthographie und Transkription moderner Drucke des Qurʾān," in* Vom Koran Zum Islam, *Groß, Markus and Karl-Heinz Ohlig, Eds. 606-641.* **Subsequent figures will refer to this as "the 1924 Cairo text" for simplicity.]**

Example 2: Post-production erasure overwritten in a 1st/7th century Qur'ān

FIGURE 3: BnF arabe 328, fol. 58v.

This example is from BnF *arabe* 328b, part of the Codex Parisino-Petropolitanus, which comprises BnF *arabe* 328a and 328b, as well as other folios that exist today in the National Library of Russia in St. Petersburg, the Vatican Library, and the Nasser D. Khalili Collection of Islamic Art in London.[3]

François Déroche has worked with this codex for many years and has described it in wonderful detail. It dates, in his opinion, to the third quarter of the 7th century, specifically to between 671 and 695 AD.[4] Dr. Altıkulaç similarly places it (referring to *arabe* 328a) in the 7th century and, like Déroche, believes it not to have been one of the copies produced by ʿUthmān, but rather a copy of one of them or a copy of a copy. Although Déroche is cautious about placing it geographically,[5] Altıkulaç sees evidence of origin in Damascus and suggests that was either copied from the codex that ʿUthmān sent there, or from a copy based upon it.[6] The Codex Parisino-Petropolitanus has many interesting distinctive features that are beyond the scope of this book.

The photograph above shows a place where the page has been erased and overwritten. Erasures were typically made by scraping off the ink with a pumice stone; this process leaves scratches on the parchment. It was often done in a very precise way following the general shape of the letters that were erased. Erasure marks are clear at this spot and I have looked at this page on two different occasions. The change has been made by a different hand and with a different nib and different ink than the rest of the writing on the page. Among other things, the *lām* (the upright extension at the right side) is less confident and more vertical in contrast with the general rightward slant of the rest of the page, including the apparent *lām* that was erased.

This correction occurs at Q42:21, and is the second of three instances of لهم *lahum* in this verse as it stands in the 1924 Cairo edition. What was first written here appears to have been *lām-he,* that is, the compound Arabic word *lahū,* "to him." It has been replaced by *lām-he-mīm,* that is, *lahum,* "to them (m.)." As such, the way this page was first written would have had a meaning, "Or do they have associates who enacted for **him** as a religion that for which Allah did not give leave?" instead of the now-standard text which says "Or do they have associates who enacted for **them**," etc. The third person singular is used in the previous verse, and as it was first written on this page, verse 21 could have been read with the "for him" referring back to the hypothetical individual mentioned in verse 20, who wishes the tillage of the Hereafter.

The way the page is written after this change corresponds at this point with the consonantal text of the 1924 Qurʾān. This correction is not the only one on this page of the manuscript; there are at least two others, including an erasure 3 lines earlier.

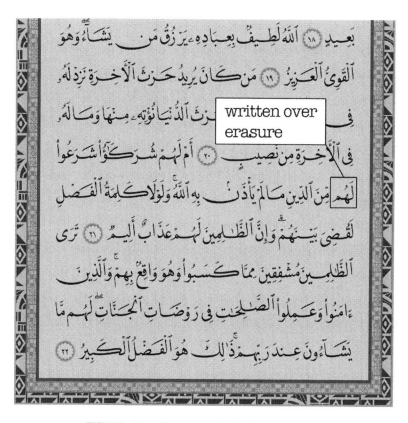

FIGURE 4: *Example 2 compared with the 1924 Cairo text*

Example 3: Multiple post-production insertions of "allāh" in several 1st/7th and 2nd/8th century Qurʾāns

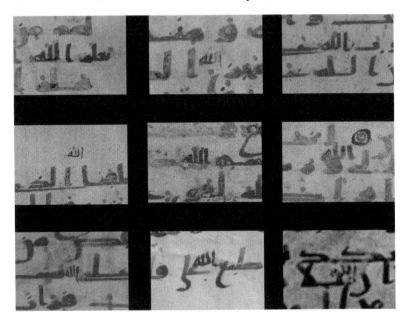

FIGURE 5: *Nine insertions of* allah *in various manuscripts (Source of San ʿāʾ image (bottom right): UNESCO CD of San ʿāʾ Qurʾāns)*

THE ABOVE FIGURE is not a single but a composite image showing nine different manuscript insertions of the word *allāh*[7] ("God") at places where the word was omitted at the time of the manuscripts' initial production. I have so far catalogued about a dozen such instances in Qurʾān manuscripts produced in the 7th and 8th centuries, most of these in the Fustat Umayyad Codex, and it has fascinated me to discover that, of all things for a scribe to "forget," *allāh* would be among them. I don't believe, actually, that *allāh* was truly forgotten in all these cases; in almost every instance shown above, Allah is the implied subject but is not grammatically necessary. This recurrence of similar corrections in different places seems to me evidence, perhaps, of a certain degree of early flexibility in the manuscripts and probably also reflects the oral nature of the transmission (since manuscripts are not produced in a vacuum) that was at some later point in time drawn toward uniformity.

Here is a description of each one of the above, from top left to bottom right:

THE "FUSTAT UMAYYAD CODEX"

Many full manuscripts have been broken up into sections and remain separated today in different libraries and museums. Such is the case with one codex that François Déroche has named the *Fustat Umayyad Codex*. He believes it could possibly be either the codex sent by al-Hajjāj to the ʿAmr mosque, or that made by ʿAbd al-ʿAzīz b. Marwān in response to this action.[8] Whatever the case, this codex apparently remained in the ʿAmr mosque for a thousand years until the early 1800s, when the various portions were acquired by Jean-Joseph Marcel and making their way to Europe.[9] The manuscript fragments now exist under four call numbers: three in Russia (Marcel 11, Marcel 13, and Marcel 15) and one in Paris (BnF *arabe* 330c).[10] This manuscript is written in the O I script style[11] and was probably produced in the first part of the 8th century AD.

The Fustat Umayyad Codex has many interesting features. Prof. Déroche has described it in in detail, and I have seen and made my own close observations of all its folios in both Paris and St. Petersburg. The interesting feature I am highlighting in this example of change (which actually consists of seven changes in this codex and two in other ones) is the apparent late standardization of a number of instances of *allāh*. Here is a description of each one in turn, with the manuscript and folio listed as well as the particular instance of *allāh* that was omitted and then inserted shown in bold:

1. NLR Marcel 11, 7v. Q33:18, *qad ya ʾlamu* **llāhu** *ʾl-mu ʿawwiqīn minkum,* "**Allah** surely knows those from among you who hinder others..." This is an erasure overwritten, but it is almost certainly the *allāh* that was missing earlier; if this was the case, the *ya ʾlamu* was erased and both words were then written in. As such, this manuscript prior to the change would have read, "**He** surely knows those from among you who hinder others..."

2. NLR Marcel 11, 8r. Q33:24, *li-yajziya* **llāhu** *ʾl-ṣādiqīn bi-ṣidqi-hum,* "In order that **Allah** might reward the truthful for their truthfulness... ." Prior to the insertion, this manuscript read, "In order that **he** might reward the truthful for their truthfulness."

3. NLR Marcel 11, 10v. Q33:73, *wa-yatūba* **llāhu** *ʿalā ʾl-mu ʾminīna wa-ʾl-mu ʾmināt,* "and that **Allah** might pardon the believing men and believing women." Prior to the insertion, this manuscript read, "And that **he** might pardon the believing men and believing women."

4. NLR Marcel 11, 12v. Q41:21, *qālū ʾanṭaqanā* **llāhu** *lladhī anṭaqa*

kulla shayʾin, "they will say, '**Allah** who gave everyone speech gave us speech.'" Prior to the insertion, this manuscript read, "they will say, '**He** who gave everyone speech gave us speech.'"

5. NLR Marcel 13, 20v. Q22:40, *yudhkaru fīhā smu llāhi kathīran,* "wherein the name **of Allah** is mentioned frequently." Prior to the insertion, this manuscript read, "Wherein the name is mentioned frequently."

6. NLR Marcel 13, 23r. Q24:51, *duʿū ʾilā llāhi wa-rasūlihī,* "they are called unto **Allah** and his Messenger." Prior to the insertion, this page looks like a nonviable reading because of the presence of the *wāw* ("and"). It is therefore not clear what might have been going on in this sentence.

7. NLR Marcel 13, 26r. Q35:11, *inna dhālika ʿalā llāhi yasīrun,* "that is indeed an easy matter for **Allah**." Prior to this insertion it is unclear how or whether this manuscript would have been read sensibly at this point.

OTHER MANUSCRIPTS

8. NLR Marcel 21, 4v, line 11. Q9:93, *wa-ṭabaʿa llāhu ʿalā qulūbihim,* "and **Allah** has placed a seal upon their hearts." Prior to this insertion, the manuscript read, "and **he** has placed a seal upon their hearts."

Marcel 21 is a horizontal fragment on parchment of 12 folios in 3 quires. It is a composite fragment, in that the third quire, folios 9-12 (two bifolios), are clearly originally from a different codex than the first two quires. As this insertion comes from folio 4, I will only describe that portion of this manuscript. Its pages measure about 17.9 cm tall by 29.5 cm wide (about 7" x 11.6"), with the text block measuring 13 cm. tall by 23 cm. wide. The script style is Déroche's A.I. This first part of Marcel 21 was likely produced in the early 8th century; the third quire may date to the 7th century. Altogether, I have noted about three dozen corrections in Marcel 21.

9. UNESCO CD of Sanʿāʾ Qurʾāns, shelf number 01-20.4. Q9:78, *wa-ʾanna* **llāha** ʿ*allāmu* ʾ*l-ghuyūb,* "and that **Allah** knows fully the things that are unseen." Prior to this insertion, this manuscript read, "and that **he** knows fully the things that are unseen."

The final *allāh* insertion shown in this example, from the bottom right of Figure 5, is found on a page from the Sanʿāʾ manuscripts. I do not have the dimensions of the page and have seen it only in a photograph, not in person as I have all the others in Example 3. The page is horizontal in format, with 22 lines on the page. It has virtually no margin, and in this regard is very similar to the earliest vertical ḥijāzī manuscripts, which also tend to make full use of the page right out to the edges. This is probably a late 7th or early 8th century manuscript.

FIGURE 6: Illustration of the allāh insertion at Q33:18 in the Fustat-
Umayyad codex as compared with the 1924 Cairo text

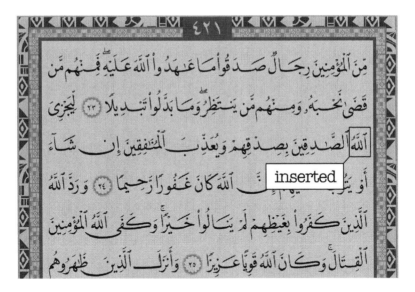

FIGURE 7: *Illustration of the* allāh *insertion at Q33:24 in the Fustat-Umayyad codex as compared with the 1924 Cairo text*

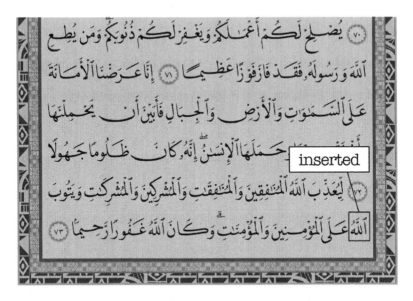

FIGURE 8: *Illustration of the* allāh *insertion at Q33:73 in the Fustat-Umayyad codex as compared with the 1924 Cairo text*

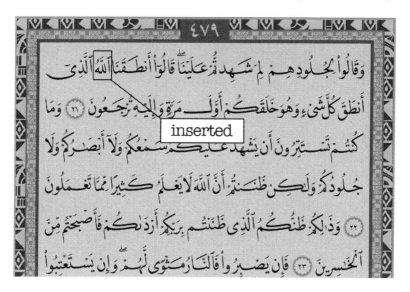

FIGURE 9: *Q41:21 in the 1924 Cairo text, showing location of the* allāh *insertion in manuscript #4 above*

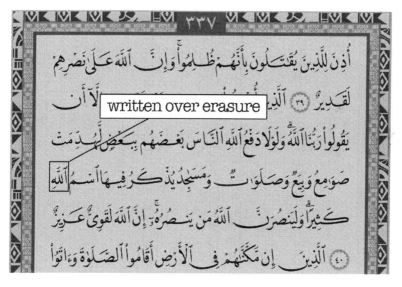

FIGURE 10: *Q22:40 in the 1924 Cairo text, showing location of the* allāh *insertion in manuscript #5 above*

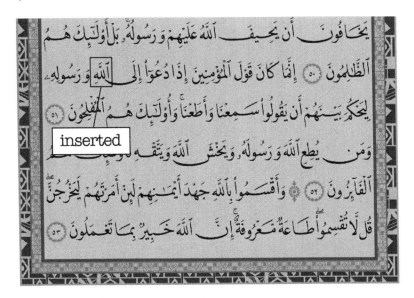

FIGURE 11: Q24:51 in the 1924 Cairo text, showing location of the allāh
insertion in manuscript #6 above

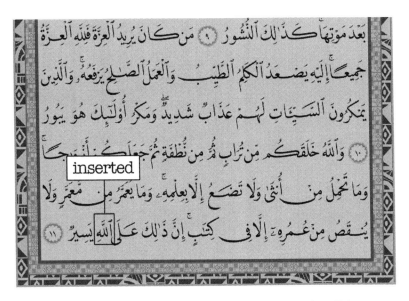

FIGURE 12: Q35:11 in the 1924 Cairo text, showing location of the allāh
insertion in manuscript #7 above

FIGURE 13: *Q9:93 in the 1924 Cairo text, showing location of the* allāh *insertion in manuscript #8 above*

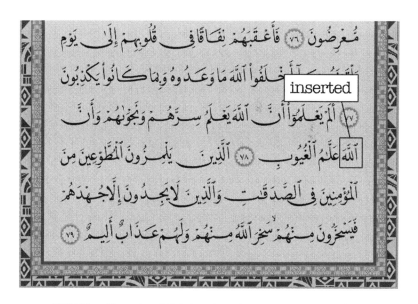

FIGURE 14: *Illustration of* allāh *insertion at Q9:78 in manuscript #9 above, showing the location in the 1924 Cairo text*

THE ABOVE NINE corrections represent about three-quarters of the simple *allāh* insertions I have noted so far. In addition to these, there are many corrections beyond simple insertions that involve *allāh*. On its face, this should not be terribly surprising, since *allāh* is one of the most common words in the Qur'ān. Still, the specific nature of the corrections above makes them worthy of attention.

Example 4: An erasure

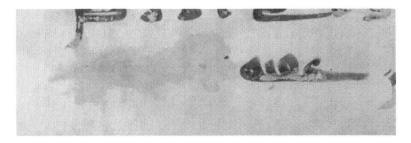

FIGURE 15: An erasure leaving a gap in Marcel 2, on the last line of the page.

This correction is found in the manuscript Marcel 2, in the National Library of Russia, on folio 30v. This is a large square Qur'ān, with pages measuring about 41 cm. (~16 in.) square. Its text block measures 33 cm. tall by 31 cm. wide (~13 in x 12 in.). Its format is similar to that of the Cairo *muṣḥaf al-sharīf*. Marcel 2 has 42 folios with 20-21 lines of script per page. It contains verse dividers in the form of vertical stacks of diagonal nib marks, as well as multi-verse dividers in the form of red medallions circled with brown ink, preceded by stacked nib marks as mentioned already. Occasionally it has multi-verse dividers in the form of a red medallion with four spikes at diagonals and petals extending right and left, up and down. These pages are written in the script style C.Ia, and this is probably an early 8th century manuscript. I've noted 26 corrections in this manuscript fragment.

The correction in this case is a simple erasure; nothing has been written to replace what was erased. A gap is left by the erasure at the end of the line, the final line on the page. The erasure follows the word عقبة *ʿāqibatu*, "the fate," of Q30:9. The word that comes next in the 1924 Cairo edition, الذين *alladhīna*, "(of) those," is the first word written on the following page of this manuscript. So, the *rasm* now aligns at this point with the 1924 Cairo text.

This verse follows a narrative that chastises disbelievers for not recognizing the signs and the fate of those who disobeyed God in the past: "Have they not travelled in the land to see what was the fate of those who preceded them? They were stauncher than them in strength, and they plowed the earth and built it up better than they themselves built it up, and their messengers came to them with the clear proofs. Allah would not wrong them but they wronged themselves."

What was erased cannot at this time be discerned, but the length and continuity of the erasure indicates a likely single word of 4-6 letters, all linked. Grammatically, assuming that the rest of the verse was read at the time of this manuscript as it is today, there are possibilities that could fit in this space. The first would be an expression of proportion such as *kullu min*, "all of," or *kathīran min*, "most of," to render "what was the fate of all those who preceded them," or "what was the fate of most of those who preceded them," respectively. Another possibility would be a noun (for example, *al-yahūd*, "the Jews," or *al-nās*, "the people") with the resulting translation, "what was the fate of the Jews who went before them," or "what was the fate of the people who went before them." To be clear, I have no indication that the erased writing said any of these things; I mention them to illustrate that there are grammatically viable possibilities.

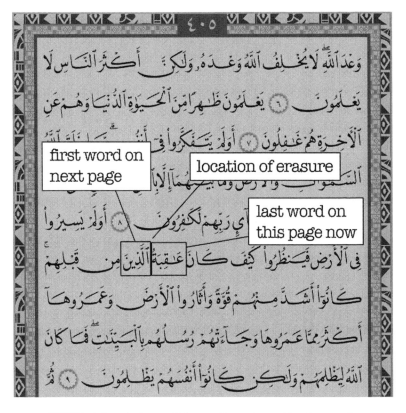

FIGURE 16: Q30:9 in the 1924 Cairo text, illustrating the Marcel 2 correction

There is one other correction on this page in Marcel 2, an insertion in the left margin. Like the one above, it has also brought the page toward conformity at that point with the *rasm* of the 1924 Cairo edition.

Example 5: A Qur'ān page, possibly 2nd/8th-3rd/9th century, containing several post-production corrections

FIGURE 17: MS.474.2003, fol. 9v. (Brubaker photo, by permission of the Museum of Islamic Art)

This page is in the Museum of Islamic Art in Doha, Qatar. Its script style is Déroche's A.I, and it is probably of 8th century production. The manuscript fragment (MS.474.2003) has about 30 physical changes over its 12 folios, and it is variant when compared with the 1924 Cairo edition.

The photograph above (Figure 17) shows part of folio 9v, a page that contains at least five instances of correction. Before discussing these, here is a general description of the script on this page.

This folio begins in the middle of Q6:91. Even as it now stands, it has a variant *rasm*; for example:

- *wa-lā* "nor" of Q6:91 is written instead as *wāw*,

"and;" the *lām- ʾalif* has been omitted. The meaning
here is thus "you and your fathers" rather than the
1924 Cairo edition's "you nor your fathers"

- What reads *mubārakun muṣaddiqu*, "[it is] blessed
  and confirms," in the 1924 Cairo edition of Q6:92 is
  written in this manuscript without the long medial
  ʾalif in the first word and also with a long *ʾalif* at the
  end of both words, to render *mubarakān
  muṣaddiqān*, apparently "a blessed and confirming
  one."

- The *wāw* "and" that precedes *li-tundhir*, "that you
  may warn," in the 1924 Cairo edition is absent on
  this page.

- What reads *ṣalātihim* (archigraphemically CLA
  BHM), "prayers," in the 1924 Cairo standard is
  written in this manuscript with a *wāw* instead of
  the medial long *ʾalif*, that is, *ṣalawātihim,*[12] or,
  archigraphemically, CLW BHM. The latter is plural;
  a slight change of meaning.

- The *aw*, "or," of Q6:93 is written in this manuscript
  as *wa*, "and," to render "he who imputes falsehood
  to Allah **and** says," instead of the 1924 Cairo
  edition's "he who imputes falsehood to Allah **or**
  says."

- The 1924 Cairo standard's *idh*, "while," of Q6:93 is
  written in this page as *idhā*, "when."

- The long *ʾalif* that is in second position of the *bāṣṭū*,
  "outstretched," of Q6:93 in the 1924 Cairo edition is
  missing on this page.

- The word ربكم *rabbikum*, "your Lord," is written
  between *allāh* and *fa- ʾinnā* of Q6:95. This does not

exist in the 1924 Cairo edition but does make grammatical sense here, reading, "That is Allah **your Lord**, how then," rather than "That is Allah, how then" as it exists in today's standard. It is interesting that the correctors of this page did not erase this word. Did they feel it belonged here?

The points above give a sense of the variant character of this manuscript. Now we will discuss the corrections on this page. There are at least five:

1) THERE IS an erasure near the end of line 3, of two words whose shadow partly remains. It occurs after the *ḥawlahā wa*, "around it, and," of Q6:92 and before the *alladhīna*, "those who," that follows it. A significant gap remains. The result at this point is a *rasm* that conforms to the 1924 Cairo standard.

2) ON THE 6th line pictured, the word عليه *ʿalayhi*, "against him," has been written over an erasure in Q6:93 following the words *bimā kuntum taqūlūn*, "for what you (pl.) used to say." However, the 1924 Cairo edition does not read *ʿalayhi* here, and moving closer to conformity might be the reason for what I believe to have been the next intervention, noted in point #3.

3) A SUBSEQUENT correction was made at Q6:93, this time in the right margin, where على الله *ʿalà allāh*, "about Allah," has been written, but oddly without erasing the *ʿalayhi* that it is apparently intended to supplant. Also, this phrase is written

next to the start of the following line, but it seems to be intended for this spot.

The more interesting thing here is that the page at this line remains out of conformity with the 1924 Cairo edition in that it includes the additional words و بالله تكفرون *takfurūna bi-llāhi wa*, "they disbelieve in Allah and," after the words بما كنتم *bimā kuntum* and تقلون *taqulūn* of this verse. That those words were not only plainly written in this manuscript here at the time of its production, but also allowed to remain in it after two rounds of correction, despite not being part of the 1924 Cairo edition, seems important.

4) ON THE 8th line pictured, the word الذين *alladhīna*, "whom," of Q6:94 has been inserted where it was at first omitted.

5) AT THE beginning of the second to last line of the page, the word يعلمون *ya'lamūna*, "they know," of Q6:97 has been written over an erasure. The shadow of what was first written can still be seen and its archigrapheme appears to be BHMW N; however, this archigrapheme renders no word in the Qur'ān. It is possible, I suppose, that the erased text was BEMHW N; this could correspond to one word, يعمهون *ya'mahūn*, "blind/dumbfounded," a word that occurs only seven times in the Qur'ān, with one of them being at the end of Q6:110, that is, in close proximity to this verse. If this were indeed what was first written here, the verse would have read "We have made plain the signs for a people who are blind." It is difficult, at this point, to make a strong opinion on this, since the new writing

covers the erasure partially. So, while possible, it is not at all clear that an ʿayin was present.

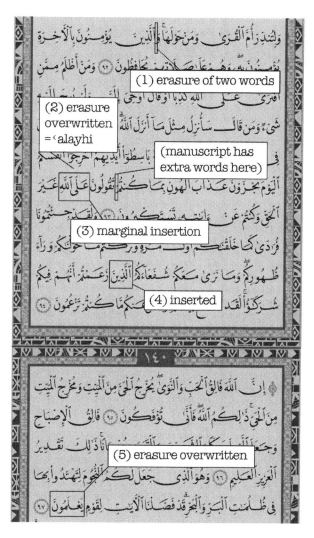

FIGURE 18: Q6:92-97 in the 1924 Cairo text, with the MS.474.2003 corrections shown

Example 6: Multiple post-production corrections in a 1st/7th century Qurʾān

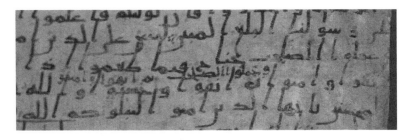

FIGURE 19: MS.67.2007.1 (Brubaker photo, by permission of the Museum of Islamic Art)

THIS FRAGMENT, and two others grouped under sequential shelf numbers, is of a similar time period and style to the Codex Petropolitanus (BnF *arabe* 328a-b, etc.) and also the Birmingham folios that Alba Fedeli brought to the world's attention, which were radiocarbon dated with a very early date range, a 95.4% probability of the animal having been last alive between 568-645 AD.[13] Several years prior to the testing of the Birmingham folios, parchment from the palimpsest Ṣanʿāʾ 1 were similarly radiocarbon dated, giving a 95% confidence date range of 578-669 AD.[14] BnF *arabe* 328 is a vertical bifolio written in Māʾil/hijāzī script.

The corrections here are found in MS.67.2007.1, in the Museum of Islamic Art in Doha. Inserted are the words *wa-ʿamilū ʾl-ṣāliḥāti thumma ttaqaw wa-ʾāmanū* of Q5:93. The main insertion has been made above the main line of text. Except possibly for the first portion, *wa-ʿamilū,* about which I have some question because of the way it is written, this insertion looks to be the work of the original scribe and was probably made soon after the time of first writing. Q5:93 has several repetitions in it, and it is not at all surprising that a scribe might have become confused and made a mistake that needed to be corrected later. This correction is thus almost certainly due to a simple copyist error at first writing.

There is one part of this insertion, however, that appears to be part of a second and later correction. It is the final *ʾalif* of *ʿamilū*, "they did," and this orthography of the third person plural ending, I think, was omitted at first correction and added later. Also, the corresponding *ʾalif* of *ʾāmanū*, "they believed," at the very end of this insertion is missing, a further odd detail, given that it is typically used elsewhere on this page and was also added in at the end of *ʿamilū*.

Finally, and perhaps most interestingly, the initial *ʾalif* of احسنوا *ʾaḥsanū*, "they did good (imperative, 3rd pl.)," was omitted at the time of first writing and was added later, but with red ink, the same ink used for the dots representing short vowels elsewhere on this page.

So, there is a lot going on in some of these manuscripts, and a close and careful examination is needed. I almost did not notice the issue with the *ʾalif* of *ʾaḥsanū* myself. There have been several times (I remember one quite clearly at the Bodleian Library in Oxford several years ago), when I have been working closely and carefully with a page for a long time and have almost been ready to move on before noticing a correction that ought to have been plainly obvious sooner. It is a reminder that patience, humility, and attention to detail is essential in this work.

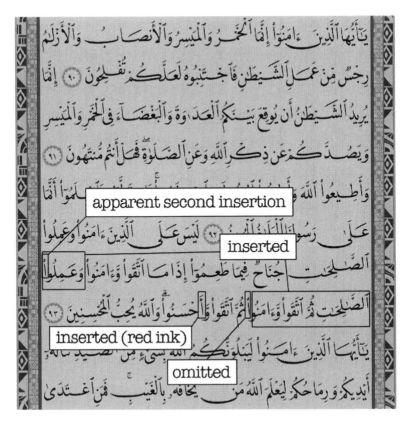

FIGURE 20: Q5:93-94 in the 1924 Cairo text, with the MS.67.2001 corrections shown

The complexity of the above situation may be taken as evidence that this manuscript was in use and was felt important enough to correct, multiple times. The issue with the red *ʾalif* is interesting because it is not a matter of orthography or reading. So, there is more work remaining to be done on this section and in this manuscript, which has layers of information to unpack.

Example 7: Post-production insertion of the words "the seven"

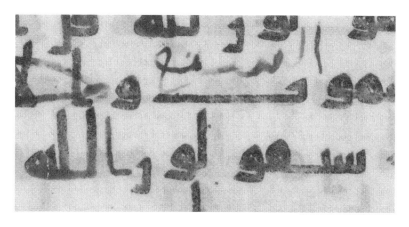

FIGURE 21: BnF arabe 327, fol. 1r.

BnF *arabe* 327, in the National Library of France, is written in Déroche's B.Ib style. A fragment of 14 folios, its pages are nearly square, 26-27 cm. (about 10.5 inches) tall and just slightly wider, with 18 lines of writing per page. It probably dates to the 8th century. I have noted nine different corrections in this manuscript, and I believe one of these was corrected more than once.

Two different corrections can be seen in Figure 21. The first is above the upper line shown, where the words السبع *al-sab ʿi*, "the seven," of Q23:86 have been added by a later scribe and in a very different script style from that of the original scribe. As first written, this portion read, "Say: 'Who is the Lord of the heavens and the Lord of the Great Throne?'" As corrected, and as it stands in the 1924 Cairo edition, it reads, "Say: 'Who is the Lord of the **seven** heavens and the Lord of the Great Throne?'"

Clearly, the verse makes sense either with or without the word; the only question is which reading reflects the original.

The number seven occurs several places in the Qur'ān, but is not a strong motif as it is, for example, inside the Bible. There is one other folio, probably 8th century but possibly late 7th, from among the San'ā' manuscripts that omits the word seven in Q9:80 where the word *does* exist in the standard text today.[15] That page, although corrected elsewhere, is not corrected at this point; its "omission"[16] was allowed by the corrector to remain. The details in that manuscript, at a verse that seems to have strong intertextual connotations, around the number seven have led me to suspect that there was something going on relating to this word "seven." Q9:80 is talking about forgiveness, and, with the inclusion of "seventy," it suddenly shares two elements with Matthew 18:21-22, "Then Peter came and said to Him, 'Lord, how often shall my brother sin against me and I forgive him? Up to seven times?' Jesus said to him, 'I do not say to you, up to seven times, but up to seventy times seven.'" To be clear, the omission at Q9:80 occurs in a different manuscript from the one pictured above, but, because of it, I find any insertion or a variant involving "seven" or "seventy" to be interesting.

The lower line pictured above also has a correction, by a different corrector, I think. It is an inserted 'alif in front of *li-llāhi* "Allah's" of Q23:87. The result does not align with the 1924 text, but it does comport with Abū 'Amr's reading (and another); it is standard in some parts of the world today. The effect is to convert the word "Allah's" to "Allah." This word is an answer to the question posed in the prior verse, "Who is the Lord of the seven heavens and the Lord of the Great Throne?" This conversion, at this particular verse, has been discussed by

Cook, who notes the resultant reading as allegedly aligning with the codex sent by 'Uthmān to Basra, as described in al-Dānī, who ascribes the insertion to Ḥajjāj.[17]

An oval mark, partially pictured, also lies over the words following this correction. It marks that the words والارض *wa-l-'arḍ*, "and the earth" (which is not present in the 1924 text) for omission, to be replaced by the inserted *al-sabʿi*.[18] Thus, "the heavens and the earth" has in this manuscript become "the seven heavens."

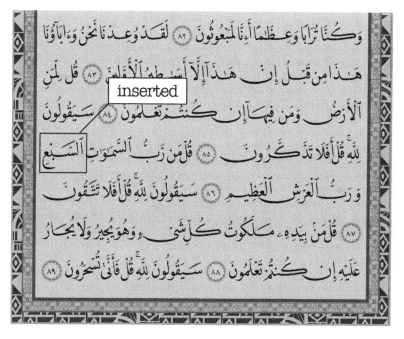

FIGURE 22: Illustration of location of correction Example 7 compared with the 1924 Cairo text

Example 8: Erasure overwritten in a 1st/7th century Qur'ān, possibly by original scribe and likely soon after original production

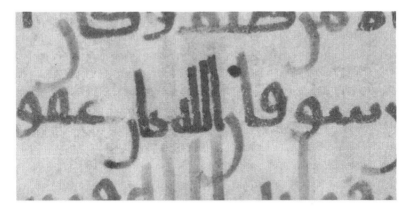

FIGURE 23: BnF arabe 330, fol. 55r.

BNF *ARABE* 330 is a fragment of 69 large vertical parchment folios, approximately 37 cm. (14.5 in.) tall by 28 cm. (11 in.) wide. It is a composite manuscript; its folios are not all from the same original Qur'ān. Prof. Déroche classified its folios under various script styles: ḥijāzī III, A.I, and B.Ib.[19] He has recently classified the portion 330c as style O I,[20] and considers it to be part of the Fustat Umayyad Codex.[21] The page shown (from 330g) above remains, for the moment, unclassified.[22] I have visited BnF *arabe* 330 twice and have noted 65 corrections among its pages.

In the example pictured above, *allāh* ("Allah") of Q4:149 has apparently been replaced by كان الله *allāhu kāna*, "Allah is," via erasure and overwriting. This change appears to be the work of the original scribe and may have happened as part of the production process (for example, after proofreading the line or the entire page when it was first written). Probably the word *kāna* was initially omitted, since the phrase *fa-ʾinna llaha ʿafuwwān qadīran*, "so surely Allah is Forgiving, Powerful," and was corrected to remedy the faulty grammar.

The verse carries the same sense with or without this word, but its inclusion is standard today. I have found no mention of an issue at this spot in the *qirāʾāt* literature.

This is not the only correction on this folio; seven lines below it there is another erasure that has been overwritten.

FIGURE 24: Illustration of location of correction Example 8 compared with the 1924 Cairo text

Example 9: Post-production insertion of "the Merciful"

FIGURE 25: BnF arabe 327, fol. 12v.

This is the second example of correction from BnF *arabe* 327. A general description of the manuscript can be found in Example 7 above.

In this case the words الرحيم *al-raḥīm*, "the Merciful," of Q42:5 were omitted at the time of production and have been added in above the line at a later time. The correction in this case appears to be the work of a different scribe. It is the last word of the verse, and completes the pair of attributes of Allah that commonly ends a verse. As first written, the verse read, "and Allah is the Forgiving." As corrected, and as is standard today, it reads, "and Allah is the Forgiving, **the Merciful.**"

There are two additional interesting things about this correction. First, it looks like it has been written with two different nibs, one very narrow and the other a little wider, though still not as wide as that which was used for the original production of this page. Second, the correction itself appears to have been rubbed out or almost erased at some point.

The verse is grammatically correct and semantically viable without the insertion, but its absence throws off the standard rhythm, as the expectation is usually for a pair of attributes of Allah at the end of a verse. Also, the first word of the pair, الغفور *al-ghafūr*, "the Forgiving," does not fit the rhyme pattern of the other verse endings in this chapter, while the inserted *al-raḥīm* does. There are a number of places in the Qur'ān where verse endings do depart from the overall rhyme pattern, and a deviation can serve a poetic purpose,[23] but it is difficult to imagine reading this verse with only the single attribute.

FIGURE 26: Illustration of location of correction Example 9 compared with the 1924 Cairo text

Example 10: Post-production mid-line insertion in a 1st/7th century hijazi manuscript

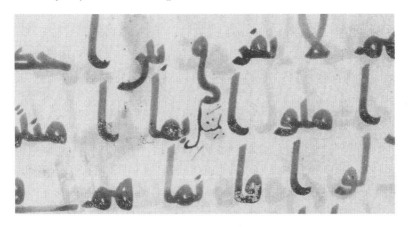

FIGURE 27: BnF arabe 331, fol. iv.

BnF *arabe* 331 is also in the National Library of France. It is a well-preserved fragment of 56 very large parchment folios, about 39.5 cm. (15.5 inches) tall by 34 cm. (13.5 inches) wide. It has about 19 lines of writing per page. Its script style has been identified by Déroche as B.Ia.[24]

In the detail of this manuscript shown above, the word مثل *mithli*, "as," of Q2:137 was omitted at first writing and then added in at a later time, with the preceding *bi*. The correction is in a very different hand using a much narrower nib; it looks almost like a modern intervention on the page. This having been said, the ink used for the insertion is very close in color and consistency to that of the original writing on this page. Probably this was just a very good match in ink, but it bears mention.

One interesting feature of this case is that the *bi* which was first written, linking forward to *mā*, has not been erased, so as it stands now it has an extra letter when compared to the 1924 Cairo text, with the portion written as امنوا بمثل بما *amanū bi-mithli bi-mā*, an apparently non-viable reading.

As this page was first written, the verse makes grammatical and semantic sense, "If they believe **in** that which you have believed," versus the 1924 Cairo text, which is approximately translated, "If they believe **similarly to** that which you have believed."

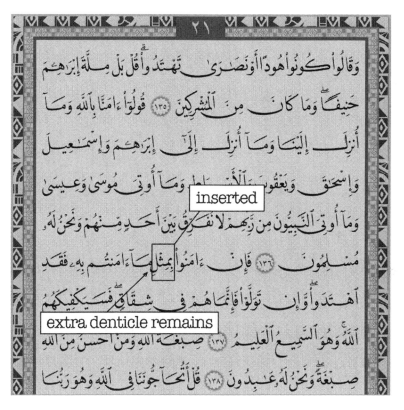

FIGURE 28: Illustration of location of correction Example 10 compared with the 1924 Cairo text

Example 11: Post-production marginal insertion of "Allah" in the Topkapı codex

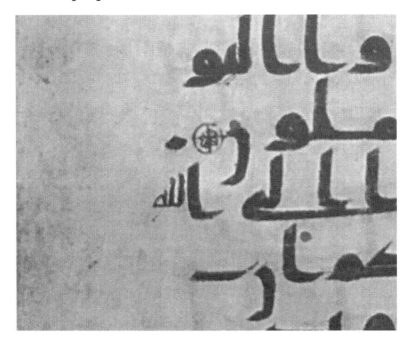

FIGURE 29: Topkapı codex, fol. 374v. (Source: Altıkulaç, Tayyar, Ed. Al-Muṣḥaf al-Sharif attributed to ʿUthmān bin ʿAffān (The copy at the Topkapı Palace Museum). Istanbul: IRCICA, 2007.)

This is a second instance of correction from the Topkapı codex, and also a further insertion involving the word *allāh*.

This insertion of *lām-lām-he* occurs near the beginning of Q66:8. As originally written, the first *allāh* of this verse was not present. This change has been made with a very small nib and probably occurred long after the first production of this manuscript. It is possible this addition is a modern intervention.

Prior to the insertion, this could have been read "Oh you who believe! Turn to a sincere repentance," were it not for the original inclusion of the *'alif* after *'ilā*. There is obviously a certain range of possibilities for some of these archigraphemes — for example, if some letters were to be pointed differently than they are today, rendering different consonants — that could open alternate readings, but the one with the most flexibility when undifferentiated has a dot underneath it in this manuscript, binding us to *bā'*. So, it is not clear to me what was intended by the original version, or whether it could have been read viably. It is worth noting, however, that the word in question is also part of a section that has been erased and overwritten in the manuscript Marcel 104 in the National Library of Russia, and that correction will be featured, among many others, in my larger forthcoming book.

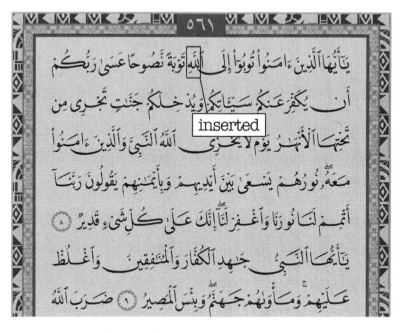

FIGURE 30: Illustration of location of correction Example 11 compared with the 1924 Cairo text

Example 12: Erasure overwritten and stretched in a 1st/7th century Qur'ān

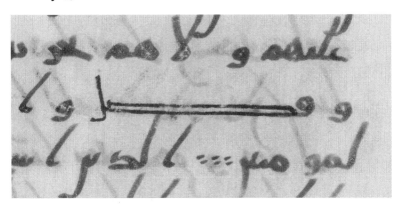

FIGURE 31: BnF arabe 328, fol. 8r.

This example shows another correction in BnF *arabe* 328a, part of the Codex Parisino-Petropolitanus. This manuscript was already introduced in Example 2.

The correction shown here is found on folio 8r, near the beginning of line 13. In it, the *ḍad-lām* of فضل *faḍlin*, "bounty," of Q3:171 has been written over an erasure. Erasure marks are clearly seen, including some of the shapes of the letters of what was first written here, among which were four upward-extending letters, the first of which is preceded by a short tooth letter. The corrector has used a different nib and ink from that which was used in first production of the page; also, the hand and angle of the script vary from that used on the rest of the page. This change is clearly a later intervention. The length of the space that is now covered by these two letters is 5.3 cm, and this would typically be occupied by five to eleven letters elsewhere on the page. There is only one other place on this page where this much space contains as few as five letters.

The result of this correction is a *rasm* that conforms at this point with that of the 1924 Cairo edition.

FIGURE 32: Illustration of location of correction Example 12 compared with the 1924 Cairo text

I have observed particular verses[25] and words[26] that are frequently corrected in Qur'ān manuscripts. The word *faḍl* is not frequently corrected, but it is of theological significance.[27] The word فضلنا *faḍalnā*, "we have favored," of Q6:86 has been written over a covering in the Cairo *muṣḥaf al-sharīf*. This is the only correction so far that I have noted for any part of Q3:171.

Example 13: Erasure overwritten, apparently changing the verb declension

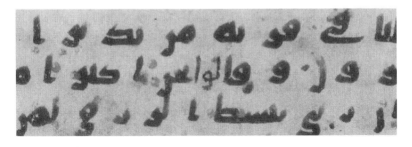

FIGURE 33: BnF arabe 340, fol. 26r.

BnF *arabe* 340 has 121 folios that are written generally in horizontal format on parchment. It is another composite fragment, meaning that its folios did not come from the same original book, but rather several. A number of its pages are in later script styles of the 10th and even 11th centuries (e.g. D and NS).[28] Déroche dates *arabe* 340(f) to the 9th century.[29] A number of these folios has been classified B.II,[30] which would be 9th century. Folios 1-12 and 13-30 (which includes the folio shown here) he has left unclassified.[31] The folio shown here, from BnF *arabe* 340(b), is probably early 9th or even 8th century.

Even though they represent different original codices, it will give readers a sense of scale to know that I have noted 91 corrections in the pages of BnF *arabe 340*.

The example above is found on 26r, one of the folios whose script style Déroche has left unclassified, in the middle of line 2. Here, the final *lām* of قال *qāla*, "he said," has been erased, and in its place *lām-wāw-alif* has been written. The result is the word قالوا *qālū*, "they (m. pl.)," of Q34:35. As it was first written, this verse read, "And **he** said, 'We are more [than you] in wealth and in children.'" As it stands now on the manuscript page, and as it exists in the 1924 Cairo edition, this verse reads, "And **they** said, 'We are more [than you] in wealth and in children.'"

This is not an extremely dramatic correction, and there are others among the pages of this fragment that are actually more interesting, but my purpose in this book is not to pick the most dramatic corrections but rather to show the range of the phenomenon. Conversions involving قال, or variations on this theme (in this case the third person plural), are among the most common types of correction in early Qur'āns.

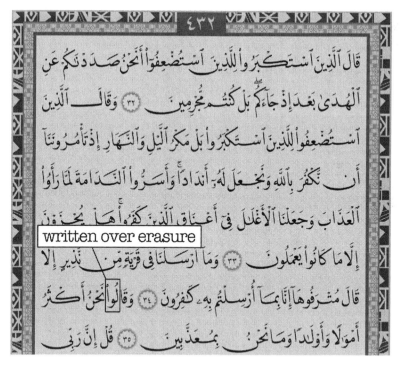

FIGURE 34: Illustration of location of correction Example 13 compared with the 1924 Cairo text

Example 14: Erasure leaving a gap in Topkapı codex

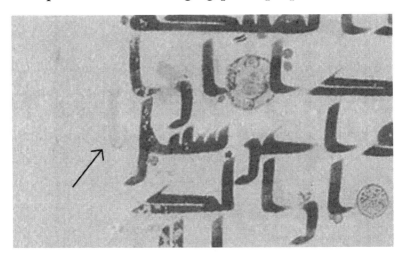

FIGURE 35: *Topkapı codex, fol. 65r, showing erasure of a single ʾalif at the end of line 11. (Source: Altıkulaç, Tayyar, Ed.* Al-Muṣḥaf al-Sharif attributed to ʿUthmān bin ʿAffān (The copy at the Topkapı Palace Museum). *Istanbul: IRCICA, 2007.)*

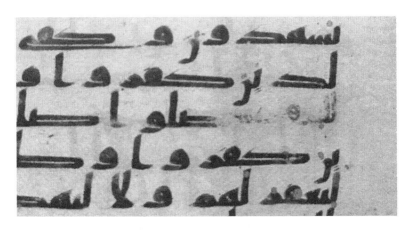

FIGURE 36: *Topkapı codex, fol. 65r, showing erasure of* llah qad *at beginning of line 12. (Source: Altıkulaç, Tayyar, Ed.* Al-Muṣḥaf al-Sharif attributed to ʿUthmān bin ʿAffān (The copy at the Topkapı Palace Museum). *Istanbul: IRCICA, 2007.)*

Here is a third example from the Topkapı codex. In this

instance, there has been an erasure of two words at the beginning of line 12, with the first letter of Allah having also been erased at the end of line 11. The shadow of what was first written remains; it is الله قد *allāhi qad*, "Allah has already," of Q4:167.

This verse is grammatically and semantically viable without the portion that has been erased. Whereas before the correction the consonantal text of this portion read, "Surely those who disbelieve and hinder from the way **of Allah** have strayed far into error," after the correction it reads, "Surely those who disbelieve and hinder from the way have strayed far into error."

The reason for this erasure is unclear, but its precision in taking out only the selected words is evident. Someone, at the time of this correction, evidently thought that those words did not belong in this place.

This is an unusual correction, as it takes the page at this point *away* from conformity with the 1924 Cairo text. Such changes represent a very small proportion of the total number of corrections I have noted; usually corrections result in a *rasm* that conforms, or that conforms more closely than it did before, with what is standard today. It is natural and reasonable to presume that a corrector felt the change that he was making to the page to be movement toward a more correct text. So in cases like these — and this one in particular is an excellent example — the question of what formed the basis for such a belief on the part of the corrector is intriguing.

It does look from the facsimile as though there has also been an erasure on line 10, just before the end of the line. I'll not describe it here, partly because I am not sure about it. It's always best to look at the manuscripts directly; even an extremely good photograph does not measure up to direct examination. Of course, as a practical matter, these objects cannot be handled by everyone, so when I go to look at them I look very closely and make detailed notes.

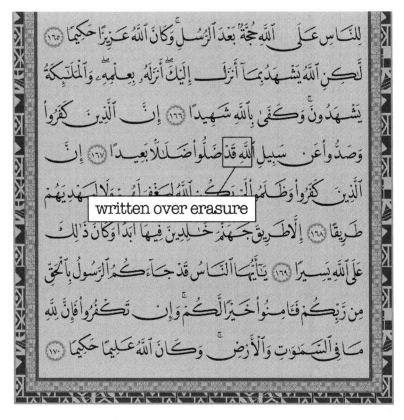

FIGURE 37: Illustration of location of correction Example 14 compared with the 1924 Cairo text

Example 15: An erasure leaving a gap in an 8th or 9th century manuscript

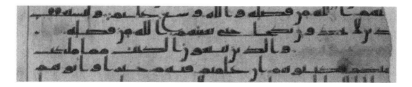

FIGURE 38: MIA.2013.19.2, verso. (Brubaker photo, by permission of the Museum of Islamic Art)

THIS IS a fragmentary partial folio on parchment in the Museum of Islamic Art in Doha, Qatar. Its writing is very similar to that of the Topkapı codex and its style is C.Ib.

In this example, there is an erasure at the end of one line and the beginning of the next. It occurs after the word فضله *faḍlihi*, "his grace," of Q24:33. The next word after the erasure is the word that follows *faḍlihi* in the 1924 Cairo edition, that is, والذين *wa-'lladhīna*, "and those who." What was first written in this space that is now empty cannot be discerned from the manuscript, as no shadow indicating the shape of the letters remains.

I have noted two manuscripts that have multi-word corrections of this verse; the other is BnF *arabe* 327, in which a long portion of text has been written over an erasure and apparently corrected more than once. That is an interesting correction, and I will certainly talk more about it in a subsequent publication. However, that correction does not cover the section of the verse at issue here; they do not overlap.

FIGURE 39: *Illustration of location of correction Example 15 compared with the 1924 Cairo text*

THE RASM of this page as it now stands aligns at this spot with that of the 1924 Cairo edition, but as this page was first written, it contained something extra. Since this manuscript is the only known copy with a correction at this point, we must wait to see if anything else emerges in future research. Perhaps there was a mere scribal error.

Example 16: A post-production insertion in the Cairo Qur'ān

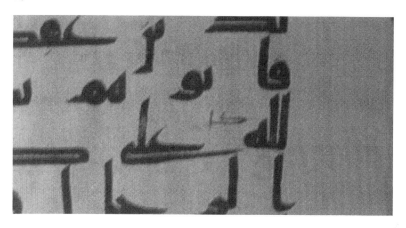

FIGURE 40: Cairo muṣḥaf al-sharīf, *fol. 109r. (Source: Altıkulaç, Tayyar, Ed.* Al-Mushaf al-Sharif attributed to Uthman bin Affan (The copy at al-Mashhad al-Husayni in Cairo). *(2 vols.) Istanbul: IRCICA, 2009.)*

This example comes from the monumental codex that is kept on display in the Ḥusaynī Mosque in Cairo. This codex is an enormous book of 1088 parchment folios. Like the Topkapı *muṣḥaf* already mentioned, it has been popularly claimed by its custodians and the governing authorities to be one of the *muṣḥaf*s of the Caliph ʿUthmān. This opinion is rejected by scholars, including Dr. Altıkulaç, who places the time of production of the Cairo *muṣḥaf* at the end of the 8th or beginning of the 9th century.[32] I will give more detail about this manuscript at the end of this chapter.

In this case, the كان *kāna*, "is," of Q4:33 was not written in this verse at the time of production of this manuscript. Though only the first two letters of this inserted word are now visible in this facsimile photograph, the full word *kāna* was presumably added here, with a very fine nib. I would like to have the opportunity to look at this manuscript directly to confirm this theory. The verse makes sense with or without the word, and its meaning is about the same in either case: "And Allah has power (lit. 'is powerful') over all things." As in many semitic languages, the verb "to be" is often not used as its sense is implied when the adjective directly following the noun it modifies. The verb can be included, but it is not grammatically necessary.

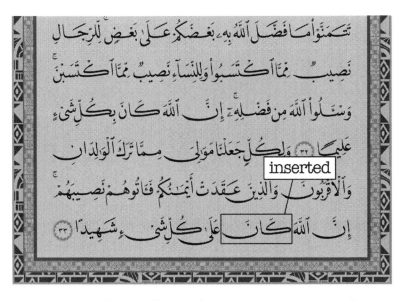

FIGURE 41: Illustration of location of correction Example 16 compared with the 1924 Cairo text

This manuscript is not the only one in which the word *kāna* has been inserted. A similar insertion of *kāna* exists in NLR Marcel 17, folio 11v, at Q4:6; however, in that case, it does not appear that as much time elapsed between original production and correction.

Example 17: A correction involving "allāh"

FIGURE 42: NLR Marcel 11, fol. 7r.

This erasure has been overwritten in Marcel 11, part of the so-called Fustat Umayyad codex, which has already been introduced under Example 3 above. Written in script style O I, this is a vertical fragment of 12 folios measuring about 36.5 cm. (~14.5 in.) tall by 31 cm. (~12 in.) wide. It has 25 lines of writing per page, and its folios are quite delicate now. This particular fragment has a very high density of corrections: I've noted 46 of them over its 12 folios. Furthermore, some of its corrections are quite dramatic.

This correction is found on 7r, in the middle of line 9. All but the first two letters of نعمة الله *ni'mata llāh*, "the favor of Allah," of Q33:9 has been written over an erasure. A different nib and ink have been used, and the writing is that of a different hand. Also, the writing has been bunched in. My impression is that this could have read *ni'matihī*, "his favor," at first; this rendering would have fit the space and would make grammatical sense here. However, this interpretation is just a reasonable conjecture; I cannot tell for sure.

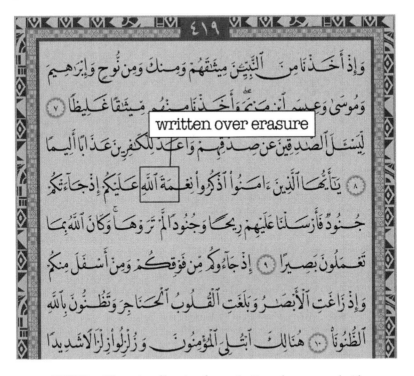

FIGURE 43: Illustration of location of correction Example 17 compared with the 1924 Cairo text

In addition to its many other corrections and this one, the 12 folios of Marcel 11 have four omissions of *allāh* that were later inserted: 33:18, 33:24, 33:73, and 41:21 — these were shown in Example 3.

Surah 33 has a fair number of corrections in the early manuscripts. Most of them are fairly small and many involve orthography. There is a more lengthy erasure overwritten at verse 73 in BnF *arabe* 340. I will discuss this and others further at a later time.

Example 18: Post-production insertion of "the hour" in a 3rd/9th-4th/10th century manuscript

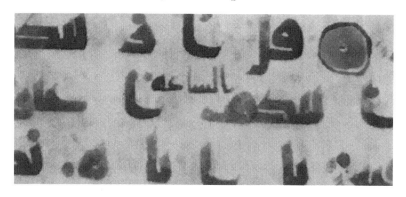

FIGURE 44: NLR Marcel 7, fol. 7r. (Brubaker photo, by permission of the National Library of Russia)

Marcel 7 is a horizontal parchment Qur'ān fragment of 10 folios. Its pages measure 17.7 cm. (~7 in.) tall by 23.3 cm. (~9 in.) wide. Its script style is probably D.IV and it is thus likely a 9th or 10th century manuscript. I have noted 8 corrections across its 10 folios, a high frequency of correction for a manuscript produced more than two centuries after the time of ʿUthmān.

In this case, the word الساعة *al-sā ʿah*, "the hour," of Q6:40 has been written in as a superscript insertion. It has been done with a very narrow nib and in a different hand. It is possible that this is a more modern correction.

This word, *al-sā ʿah*, has been corrected in other manuscripts. In BnF *arabe* 340, there is a rather lengthy erasure over-written at Q15:85 that includes the instance of this word in that verse; it is not at all clear, however, that in this case the correction had to do with this word particularly or with another. The word *sā ʿah* is also written over an erasure at Q7:34 in the

manuscript E20, located at the Institute of Oriental Manuscripts, also in St. Petersburg.

*FIGURE 45: Illustration of location of correction Example 18 compared with
the 1924 Cairo text*

Corrections involving "the hour" are interesting since this
word relates to eschatological (that is, referring to end times)
or apocalyptic themes, which an insertion such as this one
would have strengthened and clarified.[33] In both 6:40 and
15:85, the word *al-sā'ah* are eschatological references to the
hour.

Example 19: Erasure overwritten involving "allah"

FIGURE 46: NLR Marcel 5, fol. 11r. (Brubaker photo, by permission of the National Library of Russia)

Housed in the National Library of Russia, Marcel 5 is a parchment fragment of 17 folios from a large format Qur'an. Its pages measure 50 cm. (~19.5 in.) tall by 35 cm. (~14 in.) wide. Its text block measures 44 x 30 cm. (~17 x 12 in.). It has 20 lines of writing per page. Many of the letters are differentiated by diacritics, which are present in the form of fine diagonal nib marks; these seem to be original to the manuscript.

The above correction is found on folio 11 *recto*. In it, the words هو الله *huwa llāh*, "he is Allah," of Q34:27 have been written over an erasure. This is not the work of the original scribe; the ink is different and the letters are drawn in rather than written. The *huwa*, which extends into the right margin, is likely part of the same correction, though it is at least possible that it was added later. Absent the word, the verse would read at this point, "for Allah is the Mighty, the Wise;" with it, and as both this manuscript and the 1924 Cairo edition now read, it says "for **He is Allah**, the Mighty, the Wise."

It is not certain what was first written here, but my supposition is that this manuscript initially had merely *huwa,* with the subject (Allah) being implied but not explicit: "**He** is the Mighty, the Wise." The *huwa* would have, in this scenario, been erased and *allāh* or *huwa allāh* written in its place. This is conjecture but would fit the space and would make sense.

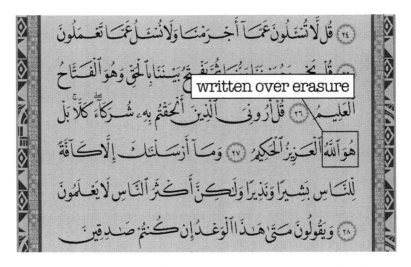

FIGURE 47: Illustration of location of correction Example 19 compared with the 1924 Cairo text

This sort of correction — that is, the replacement of an implied reference to Allah, or a pronoun referring to him, with the actual word *allāh* — is not uncommon, as should be clear by this point and in light of other examples above.

Example 20: Erasure overwritten of nearly a full line of text, involving "provision"

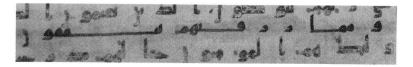

FIGURE 48: MIA.2014.491, fol. 7v. (Brubaker photo, by permission of the Museum of Islamic Art)

Located in the Museum of Islamic Art in Doha, this object is a small horizontal format bound Qurʾān fragment of nine parchment folios, measuring approximately 17.5 cm. (~7 in.) tall by 28 cm. (~11 in.) wide. Its script style is B.II.

This fragment contains several interesting corrections. Shown here is the erasure and overwriting of an entire line in the middle of folio 7. The new text is و مما رزقنهم ينفقون *wa-mimmā razaqnāhum yunfiqūna*, "and of that which We have provided them," of Q8:3, plus the initial ʾalif of the following verse. Erasure marks are quite clear on this page and the current writing on this line is somewhat stretched out to fill the space, an indication that what was first written here was longer.

The word *rizq*, "provision," is directly corrected or part of larger corrections (as is the case here) quite frequently in early Qurʾāns. It was such a prominent feature that it topped my list of frequently corrected words in early Qurʾān manuscripts in a conference paper I delivered at the International Qurʾanic Studies Association several years ago. I am not yet sure why *rizq* is so frequently corrected, that is, what the issue is, but I would not be surprised if the issue has played into the motivation for this particular instance of correction.

FIGURE 49: *Illustration of location of correction Example 20 compared with the 1924 Cairo text*

This concludes my presentation of the twenty examples. I am aware that, with Examples 3 and 5 (in particular), which contain several corrections each, I have actually shown more than twenty. My intent was to be generous, in the spirit of the old American tradition of the "bakers' dozen." Also, I wanted to take the opportunity to demonstrate some apparent patterns of correction (such as that in Example 3) that would be more difficult to see if I merely described them separately.

Another phenomenon: Covering in the Cairo Muṣḥaf?

FIGURE 50: Cairo Muṣḥaf al-Sharīf, *fol. 33v. (Source: Altıkulaç, Tayyar, Ed.* Al-Mushaf al-Sharif attributed to Uthman bin Affan (The copy at al-Mashhad al-Husayni in Cairo). *(2 vols.) Istanbul: IRCICA, 2009.)*

WHEN SURVEYING manuscripts for my doctoral dissertation, I came across some instances of what looked to me like writing that had been covered up. In an abundance of caution, I did not classify them as corrections, and even now am reluctant to do so since I have not had the opportunity in most cases to look at the manuscripts in question directly to make a very careful assessment.

Pictured above is one page of the monumental Qurʾān, in the opinion of Altıkulaç probably dating to the end of the 8th century or the beginning of the 9th. It is an interesting manuscript for a variety of reasons, not least of which is its movement between conformity with one or another of the various documented codices:

> The comparison we made between the Muṣḥafs attributed to Caliph ʿUthmān in 44 places concerning pronunciation, a superfluous or a missing letter and the structure of words leads us to think that this Muṣḥaf is not related to any of the Muṣḥafs of Caliph ʿUthman. [...T]his Muṣḥaf differs from the Medina Muṣḥaf in 14 of the 44 places, from the Mecca Muṣḥaf in 15 places, from the Kūfa Muṣḥaf in 7 places, from the Basra Muṣḥaf in 9 places and from the Damascus Muṣḥaf in 28 places. As a result, although the Cairo Muṣḥaf has common points with one or more than any one of these Muṣḥafs in each of the 44 places, it is not exactly the same as any one of them.[34]

This manuscript has more than 1,000 folios. Many of them have similar tapings that cover portions of the text. In my experience, such tape is sometimes used to repair a weak spot on the page, such as where the acidity of the ink has eaten through the parchment over the centuries, and I have observed at least one instance of such tape being applied for the purpose of repair in a manuscript fragment of a similar age and script style to the Cairo *muṣḥaf*. Indeed, on many pages of the Cairo *muṣḥaf*, parts of what is written beneath the tape extend beyond the tape edges and appear to be in alignment with what we would expect to be there when compared with the 1924 Cairo edition.

My first objective with tapings like the one above is therefore to rule out the possibility that the tape was applied merely for the purpose of page repair. Were the manuscript in front of us, we could look at the page to assess its condition, and also examine the back of the page to see if there is evidence of splitting or weakening at the spot where the tape has been applied on the reverse.

In the case of the Cairo *muṣḥaf*, I've not yet been able to survey these pages in person. I hope to be permitted to do so one day.

In absence of the opportunity for direct inspection, then, we must work from photographs, and the first thing I do after looking closely at the side with the tape is to look closely at the photograph of the reverse side of the same page. In many instances in the Cairo *muṣḥaf*, as in folio 33 pictured above, the reverse of the page appears to be perfectly sound. This observation leaves open the possibility, then, that the tape might be serving another purpose, such as selective concealing of something that is written on the page.

If the *rasm* beneath the tape of the page shown above conforms to the 1924 Cairo edition, then the covered portions would be as follows:

- Line 1 - All but the first three letters of واخرجهم من حيث *wa-ʾakhrijūhūm min ḥaythu*, "drive them out from wherever," of Q2:191
- Line 5 - All but the first two and last two letters of

فان قتلوكم *fa-ʾin-qātalūkum*, "so if you fight to kill them," of Q2:191

- Line 6 - All but the first five letters of فاقتلوهم كذلك *fa-qtulūhum kadhālika*, "then kill them (imper.), such," of Q2:191
- Line 7 - All but the last five letters of فان انتهوا *fa-ʾini-ntahaū*, "and if they desist," of Q2:192
- Line 8 - The first three letters of غفور *ghafūrun*, "forgiving," and the last three letters of رحيم *raḥīmun*, "merciful," of Q2:192
- Line 10 - All but the first letter of الدين لله *al-dīnu li-llāh*, "the religion belongs to Allah," of Q2:193
- Line 11 - All but the last letter of عدون *ʿudwān*, "enmity," of Q2:193
- Line 12 - The final two letters of بالشهر *bi-ʾl-shahr*, "in the month," of Q2:193

Until I can see what lies under the tape, I do not know what has been covered up in each case. Still, I think it is worth mentioning that these coverings exist, and in many cases seem to have been applied when there was no need of page repair, possibly to hide what was written on the page at particular points.

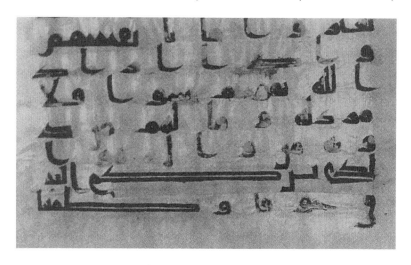

FIGURE 51: Cairo Muṣḥaf al-Sharīf, *fol. 430r. (Source: Altıkulaç, Tayyar, Ed.* Al-Mushaf al-Sharif attributed to Uthman bin Affan (The copy at al-Mashhad al-Husayni in Cairo). *(2 vols.) Istanbul: IRCICA, 2009.)*

FINALLY, there is the matter of coverings overwritten. Above is one example of this. There are many places in the Cairo *muṣḥaf* where these tapings have been written over. In the photo above, this appears to have happened in three places:

- On the first line pictured, all but the first two letters of بانفسهم *bi-'anfusihim*, "in themselves," of Q13:11 has been written on the top of such a taping.
- On the second-to-last line pictured, all but the initial *'alif* of الذى يركم *alladhī yurikum*, "he who shows you," of Q13:12 has similarly been written over a taping, and is rather stretched out. The stretching is not unusual in this manuscript, but it is more pronounced in this spot than is standard for the original scribe. It is notable that the way this section is written over the tape is missing one letter

when compared with the 1924 Cairo edition, which
has an additional *ya'* between the *ra'* and the *kaf*,
ٱلَّذِى يُرِيكُم.

- On the final line, the وطمعا *wa-ṭama 'an*, "and hope,"
of Q13:12 has also been written over a taping.

IN ALL THESE CASES, what was first written under the tape
cannot be discerned, but likely remains there and could be
seen were the tape carefully removed. It is possible that what
is written underneath matches what was written over the top,
but it is not certain that such is the case. Given the many other
instances of correction in Qur'ān manuscripts, I have not
ruled out the possibility that some of these tapings are
covering with intent to obscure a variant text or, in the case of
tapings overwritten, to change what was first written.

---

1. Altıkulaç, Tayyar, ed., *Al-Muṣḥaf al-Sharif attributed to 'Uthmān bin 'Affān (The copy at the Topkapı Palace Museum)* (Istanbul: IRCICA, 2007), 5-13.
2. Ibid., 10-13.
3. Déroche, François, *Qur'āns of the Umayyads: A first overview* (Leiden: Brill, 2014), 17.
4. Déroche, François, *La transmission écrite du Coran dans les débuts de l'Islam: Le codex Parisino-petropolitanus* (Leiden: Brill, 2009), 173; Déroche, François, *Qur'ans of the Umayyads: A first overview* (Leiden: Brill, 2014), 34.
5. Ibid.
6. Altıkulaç, Tayyar, *al-Muṣḥaf al-Sharīf Attributed to 'Uthman bin Affān: The Copy At al-Mashhad al-Husayni in Cairo* (Istanbul: IRCICA, 2009), 131-3.
7. Throughout this book, I transcribe the archigrapheme A LLH as *allāh*. The use of *ā* instead of *a* adds an element (the presumption of a long vowel) that is not, strictly speaking, present in the manuscripts.
8. Déroche, François, *Qur'ans of the Umayyads: A first overview* (Leiden: Brill, 2014), 96.

9. Déroche, François, *La transmission écrite du Coran dans les débuts de l'islam: Le codex Parisino-petropolitanus* (Leiden: Brill, 2009), 10ff.
10. Déroche, François, *Qur'ans of the Umayyads: A first overview* (Leiden: Brill, 2014), 75-7, 154-5.
11. Ibid., 105.
12. In modern convention around this particular word, even this way of writing it (i.e. with the *wāw*) is transliterated *ṣalāt,* but as per my remarks on transliteration at the front of this book, I am breaking with standard shorthand in order to precisely represent the script as it appears on the page.
13. "Birmingham Qur'an manuscript dated among the oldest in the world," University of Birmingham, posted 22 July 2015, https://www.birmingham.ac.uk/news/latest/2015/07/quran-manuscript-22-07-15.aspx
14. Sadeghi, Behnam and Uwe Bergmann, "The Codex of a Companion of the Prophet and the Qur'ān of the Prophet," in *Arabica* 57 (January 2010): 343-436. See also Sadeghi, Behnam and Mohsen Goudarzi, "Ṣanʿā 1 and the Origins of the Qur'ān," in *Der Islam* 87 (March 2012): 1-129.
15. Brubaker, Daniel, "Asking Forgiveness Seventy Times," (conference paper, Middle East Studies Association Annual Meeting, San Diego, CA, November, 2010).
16. I place *omission* in quotation marks because the fact that the particular page to which I refer was corrected but these words were not added requires us to at least consider whether these words were felt to belong here at the time and place of both original production and correction of this manuscript.
17. Cook, Michael, "The stemma of the regional codices of the Koran," in *Graeco-Arabica: Festschrift in honor of V. Christides Τιμητικοσ Τομοσ Βασιλειου Κρηστιδη* (Athens: Graeco Arabica, 2004), 93-4. There is more to say about this, as this particular change reflects something that has been discussed extensively in the literatures from the time. For the purposes of this book, however, it is enough to know this.
18. Thanks to Marijn van Putten for pointing out this explanation. I have looked at this correction for years — of course my attention is on thousands of pages and not intensely upon this one alone — without realizing that this was the function of the oval mark here.
19. Déroche, François, *Catalogue des manuscrits arabes : deuxième partie : manuscrits musulmans : tome I, 1* (Paris: Bibliothèque nationale, 1983), 63-69.
20. Déroche, François, *Qur'ans of the Umayyads: A first overview* (Leiden: Brill, 2014), 80.
21. Ibid., 76.
22. Its style is very close to that of CBL Is 1615 I/II in Dublin, with hand almost identical, van Putten has observed. (personal communication)

23. Stewart, Devin, "Divine Epithets and the *Dibacchius: Clausulae* and Qur'anic Rhythm," in *Journal of Qur'anic Studies* 15.2 (2013): 22-64. Stewart has done good work on rhyme patterns, asking whether current readings may in some cases not be the original readings. I was riveted when I first heard him present a paper on this several years ago, and I believe the line of inquiry holds potential as an item in the toolbox during the coming years of manuscript research.

24. Déroche, François, *Catalogue des manuscrits arabes : deuxième partie : manuscrits musulmans : tome I, 1* (Paris: Bibliothèque nationale, 1983), 67.

25. Brubaker, Daniel, "Frequently Corrected Verses In Early Qur'ān Manuscripts," (paper presented at the Annual Meeting of the European Association of Biblical Studies, Leuven, Belgium, July 2016).

26. Brubaker, Daniel, "Corrections involving the word *rizq* ("provision") in early Qur'āns," (paper presented at the Annual Meeting of the International Qur'anic Studies Association, San Antonio, TX, November 2016).

27. Rubin, Uri, "Meccan trade and Qur'ānic exegesis (Qur'ān 2:198)," in *Bulletin of the School of Oriental and African Studies, University of London* 53 no. 3 (1990), 421-428.

28. Déroche, François, *Catalogue des manuscrits arabes : deuxième partie : manuscrits musulmans : tome I, 1.* (Paris: Bibliothèque nationale, 1983), 109, 120, 131, 138.

29. Déroche, François. *The Abbasid Tradition: Qur'ans of the 8th to the 10th Centuries AD* (London: Nour Foundation, 1992), 54-55.

30. Déroche, François, *Catalogue des manuscrits arabes : deuxième partie : manuscrits musulmans : tome I, 1.* (Paris: Bibliothèque nationale, 1983), 69.

31. Ibid., 147.

32. Altıkulaç, Tayyar, *al-Mushaf al-Sharīf Attributed to ʿUthman bin Affān: The Copy At al-Mashhad al-Husayni in Cairo*, 2 vols. (Istanbul: Organisation of the Islamic Conference Research Centre for Islamic History, Art, and Culture (IRCICA), 2011), 124-5.

33. Rahman, Fazlur, *Major Themes of the Qur'an* (Chicago: The University of Chicago Press, 2009), 106ff; Cook, David, *Contemporary Muslim Apocalyptic Literature* (Syracuse: Syracuse University Press, 2005), 8-9.

34. Altıkulaç, Tayyar, *al-Mushaf al-Sharīf Attributed to ʿUthman bin Affān: The Copy At al-Mashhad al-Husayni in Cairo*, 2 vols. (Istanbul: Organisation of the Islamic Conference Research Centre for Islamic History, Art, and Culture (IRCICA), 2011), 124-5.

3
___

CONCLUSIONS

The Qur'ān has been, and continues to be, consequential in the affairs of men. In many parts of the world, it is a source of regional, cultural, and spiritual pride inextricably intertwined with every part of life. It is also an object of history related to one of the most dramatic and enduring movements of political conquest and colonization in the history of the world. It claims internally (e.g. Q2:1) to be revelation from God, and was also claimed as such by Muhammad himself. Furthermore, as a piece of writing (Arabic *kitāb*) with poetic and linguistic nuance, allusions to events and details of its time as well as to the biblical scriptures (Hebrew Bible and New Testament) and apocryphal writings, it contains theological and historical themes intertwined in complex ways. For all these reasons and more, it is an object that has attracted scholarly study from many different directions.

Leaving aside for the moment devotional considerations — because these are generally outside the scope of an academic inquiry — there are many ways to approach the history of the Qur'ān. For example, there is analysis through the lens of secondary literatures, both Arab/Muslim sources[1] and others,[2] both of which can carry special problems, including internal or external contradictions;[3] there is linguistic[4] and poetic or chiastic[5] analysis of the words and word groupings[6] of the Qur'ān itself, or of the presence of foreign words;[7] there is the Qur'ān's self-referentiality,[8] there is study of the historical content and clues in the text of the Qur'ān, such as places, people, and references to historical events and topography,[9] there is consideration of the theological and legal themes and motifs of the Qur'ān in context of its time and place of delivery;[10] and more.

Then, there is analysis of the material history,[11] which includes physical traces of Qur'ān passages, such as in rock inscriptions or on monuments from the early time periods. This includes consideration of the political circumstances in the period following the lifetime of Muhammad.[12]

Factoring large in the material history, of course, is the manuscripts, which serve as witnesses to the both their time of first production and also to the time (if applicable) of correction.

In the preceding pages, I have shown examples of corrections from Qur'ān manuscripts that were produced in the first several centuries after the death of Muhammad. As stated earlier, I did not choose the most dramatic examples to present here, but rather a good group of samples to introduce the range of the phenomenon. In order to provide readers the most value, I've generally decided not to pick corrections that I've judged to be the result of correcting a mere scribal mistake from the time of first production; the one exception in this book is (possibly) Example 8. Among all the corrections I've documented so far in my research, simple scribal error does account for some of them, and it is important for readers to understand that this explanation is the first factor I consider when trying to discern the cause. These manuscripts were written by human beings, not machines, and so ordinary human error must always be taken into account.

WHAT DOES the existence of these corrections mean? It is an open-ended question with many possible answers. Here are a few of my thoughts:

First, although it seems to have been reasonably demonstrated by now that (with the exception of the lower layer of the San'ā' palimpsest) most surviving Qur'ān manuscripts bear the signs of having been produced following a campaign of standardization basically consistent with that reported to have been directed by the third caliph, it is also clear that there existed *some* differences of perception about the correct words of the Qur'ān text at the times most of these manuscripts were produced, which were later revisited when these perceptions changed or standardization became more thorough. It is not impossible that some of these varying perceptions would have been tied to certain geographic regions or locales. This perceived flexibility exceeds the bounds of what is reported in the *qirā'āt* literature.

Second, these differences of perception were not confined to the earliest decades after Muhammad's death, but there was some flexibility extending for several centuries after. The flexibility does not appear to have been great. For example, with few exceptions like the 7th century Sanʿāʾ and Birmingham palimpsests, we do not usually see the correction of very large portions of Qurʾān text in the manuscripts. This degree of apparent flexibility that has limits seems to fit very well with what is seen elsewhere, such as the inscriptions in the Dome of the Rock which suggest to Chase Robinson and Stephen Shoemaker a certain instability in the text of the Qurʾān through the time of its completion in 691/2 AD, during the reign of the caliph ʿAbd al-Malik,[13] and, to the larger point, the variations requiring later correction in the manuscripts would be consistent with what Nicolai Sinai has termed the 'emergent canon model,' the hypothesis that "the Qurʾānic text, in spite of having achieved a recognizable form by 660, continued to be reworked and revised until c. 700."[14] Of course, such a model, i.e. complete closure of the quranic "canon" around 700, would still fail to account for manuscripts being produced after this time that still required later correction, unless of course every one of these were to be attributed only to orthographic developments, standard qirāʾāt variations, or scribal error at first production, a scenario that does not appear to be the case.

Third, partial correction suggests a movement toward a standard over time, a gradual process rather than a sudden complete standardization. By partial correction, I mean places where one aspect of the writing on a page was brought to conformity with the 1924 Cairo *rasm* but another part of the writing remained uncorrected. Of course, this surmise suggests that the corrector, when noting and revising one aspect of the writing on the page that he perceived to be deviant, passed over another that he presumably did not see to be incorrect.

A dominant traditional view about the Qurʾānʾs early transmission and preservation held that orality was the primary factor, and the ability of even modern children to memorize the entire Qurʾān from an early age is held forth as evidence that the same was the practice during the time of Muhammad and the centuries following. Indeed, there is little reason to doubt that oral transmission played a significant role in those early years. However, the existence of manuscripts attest also to a tradition of written transmission, and features of the manuscripts also suggest the practice of scribal copying from an exemplar.[15] That is, they looked at an existing copy in order to make a new copy, rather than either writing from memory or writing from hearing a recitation.[16] So, it is more likely that orality was part of the picture but that the major transmission of the book was not purely oral, an environment that Sadeghi and Bergmann have termed "semi-orality."[17]

A reconstruction of the physical history of the manuscripts and their relationship to both the oral tradition(s) and to one another is one goal of this work. There is, in particular, the hope of grouping manuscripts into families based upon close analysis and their textual features; this area of research is called *stemmatics*, and it highlights the familial relationship from parents (the exemplar) to children (the copies), grandchildren, cousins, and so forth. It should come as no surprise that this biological model should make use of methods and tools employed in similar work in the area of biology, and Alba Fedeli, for example, has been conducting analysis in this way.[18] The larger idea is one that has long been employed in biblical textual criticism and is well-developed in that field. Nor is it a novel concept when it comes to the Qurʾān manuscripts; classifications of these objects into families was proposed by Theodore Nöldeke as early as 1860,[19] and others have used distinctive features as a means of grouping manuscripts according to relational proximity.[20]

Clearly, the above observations bear only upon the transmission of the Qurʾān. That is to say, they do not have anything to say about questions of whether Muhammad received revelation or whether this revelation was from God; rather, they speak only to what happened later as the community of believers preserved and passed along what he delivered to them.

The mere existence of corrections in manuscripts is not the end of the story but a piece of the picture that must be taken into account when assessing what was being transmitted, in this case the words of what came to be understood by believers in Muhammad's apostleship to be a set of revelations from God. A manuscript is a physical record of a text; it is a medium of transmission and of preservation. We have many ways of transmitting and preserving information in recent years and today: print, photography, magnetic recordings such as cassette and VHS tapes, CDs and DVDs, digital archives, and of course (as in the 7th century) the handwritten document. In each case there is the possibility of noise or distortion caused by either human error or the limitations of the medium itself, but not every variation between records is necessarily the result of human error or the limitations of the medium. The work of a manuscript researcher is work in the real world of objects, using judgment to discern what is noise and what is meaningful information. I have drawn only a few conclusions here but expect that in the end, the greatest value of this book will have been the opportunity for reflection that the photographs and descriptions has provided you.

Certainly, there is much more to be said, and a great amount of material remains for further scholarly research. I will continue as I am able and hope others will also.

---

1. These include early literatures that fall into various categories: *tafsīr* (commentary), *tarīkh* (history), *sīra* (biography - i.e. of Muhammad), *rijāl* (literally "men," it is literature about the lives, lineages, and reputations for truthfulness and character of the people who were involved in transmitting traditions), *ḥadīth* (accounts of "what happened," organized topically and in discrete bits of information as reportedly passed from person to person until being collected and written down by the ḥadith collector, *maghāzī* (histories of raids and conquests), *fiqh* (legal texts rooted in the teachings of Muhammad and the Qur'ān), to name a few. Needless to say, the earlier ones tend to carry a special weight with scholars even if they are not in every case the most popular devotionally. Also, there are some works that, for various reasons, are considered to be more authoritative than others. Even the most authoritative works are not without their problems, and this is partly because all of these works tend to be separated from the events they describe by more than a century.

2. For example: Hoyland, Robert G., *Seeing Islam as others saw it: a survey and evaluation of Christian, Jewish, and Zoroastrian writings on early Islam* (Princeton: The Darwin Press, 1997).

3. Rippin, Andrew, "Al-Zuhrī, *Naskh al-Qur'ān* and the problem of early *tafsīr* texts," in *Bulletin of the School of Oriental and African Studies, University of London* 47 no. 1 (1984), 22-43; Donner, Fred McGraw, *The Early Islamic Conquests,* (Princeton: The Princeton University Press, 1981); Motzki, Harald, "Whither *Ḥadīth* Studies?" in *Analysing Muslim Traditions: Studies in legal, exegetical, and maghāzī ḥadīth* (Leiden: Brill, 2010), 47-124; Crone, Patricia, *Meccan Trade and the Rise of Islam* (Piscataway: Gorgias Press, 2004); Noth, Albrecht, *The early Arabic historical tradition: A source-critical study* (Princeton: The Darwin Press, 1994); Neuwirth, Angelika, "Qur'an and History — a Disputed Relationship: Some reflections on Qur'anic History and History in the Qur'an," in *Journal of Qur'anic Studies* 5 no. 1 (2003), 1-18; Crone, Patricia, "How did the quranic pagans make a living?" in *Bulletin of the School of Oriental and African Studies, University of London* 68 no. 3 (2005), 387-399.

4. Luxenberg, Christoph, *The Syro-Aramaic Reading of the Koran: A contribution to the decoding of the language of the Koran* (Berlin: Verlag Hans Schiler,

2007); Durie, Mark, *The Qur'an and its biblical reflexes* (Lanham: Lexington Books, 2018).

5. Cuypers, Michel, *The Banquet: A reading of the fifth sura of the Qur'an* (Miami: Convivium Press, 2009); Cuypers, Michel, *A Qur'ānic Apocalypse: A reading of the thirty-three last sūrahs of the Qur'ān* (Atlanta: Lockwood Press, 2018); Stewart, Devin, "Divine Epithets and the *Dibacchius: Clausulae* and Qur'anic Rhythm," in *Journal of Qur'anic Studies*, 15.2 (2013), 22-64; Rippin, Andrew, "The poetics of Qur'ānic punning," in *Bulletin of the School of Oriental and African Studies, University of London* 57 no. 1 in Honour of J. E. Wansbrough (1994), 193-207.

6. Bannister, Andrew G., *An Oral-Formulaic Study of the Qur'an* (Lanham: Lexington Books, 2014); Witztum, Joseph, "Variant Traditions, Relative Chronology, and the Study of Intra-Quranic Parallels," in *Islamic Cultures, Islamic Contexts: Essays in honor of Professor Patricia Crone,* ed. Behnam Sadeghi, Asad Q. Ahmed, Adam Silverstein, and Robert Hoyland (Leiden: Brill, 2015); Durie, Mark, "Phono-semantic matching in Qur'ānic Arabic," (unpublished paper, Arthur Jeffery Centre for Islamic Studies, Melbourne School of Theology).

7. Jeffery, Arthur, *The Foreign Vocabulary of the Qur'ān* (Leiden: Brill, 2007).

8. Madigan, Daniel A., *The Qur'ân's self-image: Writing and authority in Islam's Scripture* (Princeton: Princeton University Press, 2001).

9. Zellentin, Holger Michael, *The Qur'ān's Legal Culture: The* Didascalia Apostolorum *as a Point of Departure (*Tübingen: Mohr Siebeck, 2013).

10. Dost, Suleyman, "An Arabian Qur'ān: Towards a theory of peninsular origins," (PhD diss., University of Chicago, June 2017); "Geiger, Abraham, *Was hat Mohammed aus dem Judenthume aufgenommen?* (Berlin: Parerga, 2005); Reynolds, Gabriel Said, *The Qur'ān and Its Biblical Subtext* (Abingdon: Routledge, 2010); Reynolds, Gabriel Said, ed., *The Qur'ān in Its Historical Context* (Abingdon: Routledge, 2008); Reynolds, Gabriel Said, ed., *New Perspectives on the Qur'ān: The Qur'ān in its historical context 2* (Abingdon: Routledge, 2011); Zellentin, Holger Michael, *The Qur'ān's Legal Culture: The* Didascalia Apostolorum *as a Point of Departure (*Tübingen: Mohr Siebeck, 2013).

11. Small, Keith E., *Textual Criticism and Qur'ān Manuscripts* (Lanham: Lexington Books, 2011); Fedeli, Alba, "Early Qur'ānic manuscripts, their text, and the Alphonse Mingana papers held in the Department of Special Collections of the University of Birmingham," (PhD diss., University of Birmingham, 2014); Powers, David, *Muḥammad is not the father of any of your men* (Philadelphia: University of Pennsylvania Press, 2009); Puin, Elisabeth, "Ein früher Koranpalimpsest aus Ṣanʿāʾ (DAM 01-27.1)," in *Schlaglichter: Die beiden ersten islamischen Jahrhunderte,* ed. Groß, Markus and Karl-Heinz Ohlig, (Berlin: Verlag Hans Schiler, 2008); Dutton, Yasin, "Some Notes on

the British Library's 'Oldest Qur'an Manuscript' (Or. 2165)," in *Journal of Qur'anic Studies* 6 no. 1 (2004), 43-71; Sadeghi, Behnam and Uwe Bergmann, "The Codex of a Companion of the Prophet and the Qur'ān of the Prophet," in *Arabica* 57 (2010), 343-436; Rezvan, E., "New folios from ''Uthmānic Qur'ān' I. (Library of Administration for Muslim Affairs of the Republic of Uzbekistan)," in *Manuscripta Orientalia* 10 no. 1 (2004). These are just a sampling from a much wider pool of work, including works cited earlier in this book.

12. Kohlberg, Etan, and Mohammad Ali Amir-Moezzi, eds., *Revelation and Falsification: The* Kitāb al-qirā'āt *of Aḥmad b. Muḥammad al-Sayyārī (Critical Edition)* (Leiden: Brill, 2009; Modarressi, Hossein, "Early Debates on the Integrity of the Qur'ān: A Brief Survey," in *Studia Islamica* 77 (1993), 5-39. There were early debates, for example, in which it was alleged that the commonly accepted text of the Qur'ān had been corrupted. The book mentioned here is a critical edition of one such work from the 9th century AD.

13. Sinai, Nicolai, "When did the consonantal skeleton of the Qur'ān reach closure?" in *Bulletin of the School of Oriental and African Studies* 77 (2014), 273-292.

14. Ibid. 6.

15. Clues that a manuscript has been copied by looking at another manuscript include mistakes such as *haplography* (omitting a word or phrase) or *dittography* (writing the same word or phrase twice) due to *parablepsis* (looking aside when copying, for example, to fill the ink in a nib). There are numerous instances of correction in early Qur'ān manuscripts that rectify this kind of mistake.

16. This latter practice, writing from recitation, could be discerned when, for example, letters that sound the same but look different when written are interchanged. Such a mistake would not be made if the scribe was copying from an earlier manuscript. This sort of mistake is not common in Qur'ān manuscripts; in fact, no example of it comes to mind.

17. Sadeghi, Behnam and Uwe Bergmann, "The Codex of a Companion of the Prophet and the Qur'ān of the Prophet," in *Arabica* 57 (2010), 345.

18. Fedeli, Alba, and Andrew Edmondson, "Early Qur'anic Manuscripts and their Networks: a Phylogenetic Analysis Project," (pre-circulated paper for Conference "Qur'anic Manuscript Studies: State of the Field," Budapest, May 2017, after the research project *Early Qur'ānic Manuscripts and their Relationship as Studied Through Phylogenetic Software* at the Central European University, Budapest).

19. Cook, Michael, "The stemma of the regional codices of the Koran," in *Graeco-Arabica Festschrift in Honour of V. Christides Τιμητικοσ Τομοσ Βασιλειου Χρηστιδη, Volumes IX-X.* ed. George Livadas. (Athens: Graeco-Arabica, 2004), 89-104.

20. George, Alain, "Coloured Dots and the Question of Regional Origins in Early Qur'ans (Part I)," in *Journal of Qur'anic Studies* 17.1 (2017), 1-44; van Putten, Marijn, "'The Grace of God' as evidence for a written Uthmanic Archetype: The importance of shared orthographic idiosyncrasies," in *Bulletin of the School of Oriental and African Studies* (forthcoming).

INDEX OF QUR'ĀN VERSES REFERENCED

2:137 (62-3); **2:191-3** (85, 87-8); **3:171** (66-7); **4:6** (76-7); **4:33** (75-6); **4:149** (58-9); **4:167** (70-2); **5:93** (52-4); **6:40** (79-80); **6:86** (67); **6:91-97** (47-51); **7:34** (79-80); **8:3** (83-4); **9:72** (28-30); **9:78** (34, 38-9, 43); **9:80** (56); **9:93** (34, 38, 43); **13:11-12** (89-90); **15:85** (78-80); **22:40** (34, 37, 41); **23:86** (55-7); **23:87** (56-7); **24:33** (73-4); **24:51** (34, 37, 42); **30:9** (44-6); **33:9** (78-79); **33:18** (34, 36, 39); **33:24** (34, 36, 40); **33:73** (34, 36-7, 40); **34:27** (81-2), **34:35** (68-69); **35:11** (34, 37, 42); **41:21** (34, 37, 41); **42:5** (60-1); **42:21** (31-3); **66:8** (64-5)

FURTHER READING

Below is a partial list of recent books specifically dealing with Qur'ān manuscripts. Some may be challenging for a non-specialist. My mention is not an endorsement of every position, theory, or conclusion of the authors, but all are serious scholars engaging substantively with the subject.

Baker, Colin F. *Qur'an manuscripts: calligraphy, illumination, design.* London: The British Library, 2007.

Blair, Sheila S. *Islamic calligraphy.* Edinburgh: Edinburgh University Press, 2008.

Cellard, Eléonore. *Codex Amrensis I* (French and Arabic). Leiden: Brill, 2018.

Déroche, François. *Qur'ans of the Umayyads.* Leiden: Brill, 2014.

George, Alain. *The Rise of Islamic Calligraphy*. London: SAQI, 2010.

Hilali, Asma. *The Sanaa Palimpsest: The Transmission of the Qurʾan in the First Centuries AH*. Oxford: Oxford University Press, 2017.

Powers, David. *Muḥammad is not the father of any of your men*. Philadelphia: University of Pennsylvania Press, 2009.

Sinai, Nicolai. *The Qurʾan: A Historical-Critical Introduction*. Edinburgh: Edinburgh University Press, 2017.

Small, Keith. *Textual Criticism and Qurʾān Manuscripts*. Lanham: Lexington Books, 2011.

I further recommend the chapters from the following authors that are contained, among other places, in the German Inârah volumes edited by Karl Heinz-Ohlig and Markus Groß:

Alba Fedeli

Thomas Milo

Elisabeth Puin

Gerd-R Puin

Keith Small

Others who have published important journal articles, but not yet books, on Qurʾān manuscripts include notably Yassin Dutton, Mohsen Goudarzi, Efim Rezvan, Behnam Sadeghi, Ahmad Al-Jallad, Michael Marx, and Marijn van Putten. To this list could be added most of the authors of books above.

Finally, I mention one additional recently-published book that does not relate directly to the manuscripts, but which engages in fine linguistic and thematic analysis that may have some bearing on some of the things we see going on in them:

Durie, Mark. *The Qurʾan and Its Biblical Reflexes: Investigations Into the Genesis of a Religion.* London: Lexington Books, 2018.

GLOSSARY

A.H. (or AH) — the abbreviation for *Anno Hegirae,* "Year of the Hijrah," a designation of a date given according to the Islamic calendar, which counts lunar years from the time of Muhammad's emigration from Mecca to Medina in 622 AD. Centuries are often given in AD/AH format, for example "7th/1st century," meaning the 7th century AD, which is also the 1st century AH.

archigrapheme — a mark which can represent different phonemes (sounds). In this context it refers to unpointed Arabic letters, which, for lack of diacritics, were often ambiguous.

aya — a verse of the Qurʾān

bifolio — a sheet folded in the middle so as to form two folios in a bound book. Several bifolios are usually stacked and sewn together to form a quire.

codex — a book (i.e. multiple pages bound at one edge). The Arabic word for codex/book is *muṣḥaf* (pronounced "moos-hoff," NOT "mush-off")

colophon — a statement, usually included at the end of the book, that contains details about its production. In a Qurʾān manuscript, a colophon might include the name of the calligrapher, the date the project was completed, and perhaps the name of the patron who commissioned it. Unfortunately, the earliest Qurʾān manuscripts do not include colophons.

consonantal skeletal text — the Arabic *rasm,* that is, the core structure of written Arabic without any dots or other marks to disambiguate letters

diacritics — the graphic marks (usually dots today) that distinguish an otherwise ambiguous consonant. In Arabic, for example, three dots above a consonantal tooth indicate the letter *thā ʾ*, two dots above indicate a *tā ʾ*, one dot above indicates *nūn*, one dot below indicates *bā ʾ,* and two dots below indicates *yā ʾ.* There are many other examples.

folio — a page in a codex. A folio has a *recto* (front) side and a *verso* (back) side.

grapheme — the smallest unit of a writing system in a language. This term is relevant to understanding the word *archigrapheme* above.

hadith — a report that has been passed from person to person over time before being written down. Hadith typically tell of things Muhammad said or did, approved or disapproved, or similar things that his companions did or said. Separate hadith reports have been gathered into authoritative collections.

manuscript — a handwritten document

orthography - from the Greek meaning "right writing," this refers to the rules for correctly writing a word, particularly its spelling

parchment — animal skin prepared to receive writing. Parchment is sometimes also called *vellum;* they are not exact synonyms, but the terms are often used interchangeably.

qibla — the direction of Islamic prayer, today toward Mecca

quire — a section of a book consisting, usually, of several bifolios stacked and sewn together in the middle. In traditional bookbinding, and even in quality bindings today, a number of quires are first produced and then sewn or glued together to make a complete book.

rasm — an Arabic word describing the bare consonantal Arabic text. Full written Arabic today has marks representing consonants, marks representing long vowels, and sometimes marks to represent short vowels. The *rasm* refers to the first two items, but not to the last one.

recto — the front side of a folio in a book, abbreviated "r"; when referring to manuscripts in this book, for example, 26r means "26 recto," or the front side of the 26th folio. The other side is called "verso."

surah — a chapter of the Qurʾān

script grammar — a term coined in 2002 by Thomas Milo to refer to slight variations in the consonantal skeletal text that permits disambiguation of some consonants even in the absence of dots

verso — the back side of a page in a book, abbreviated "v"; when referring to manuscripts in this book, for example, 26v means "26 verso," or the back side of the 26th folio. The other side is called "recto."

ABOUT THE AUTHOR

Dr. Brubaker examining folios of a 7th century Qur'ān in the Ṣabaḥ Collection of the Dar Museum, Kuwait, 2015.

DANIEL BRUBAKER became fascinated by corrections in Qur'ān manuscripts during his Ph.D. work at Rice University, so fascinated that he chose to make these his prime focus. His dissertation, titled "Intentional Changes in Qur'ān Manuscripts" (2014), is the first extensive survey of physical corrections in early written Qur'āns. Its contents and additional material are forthcoming. This is Brubaker's first book.

facebook.com/drbruı

twitter.com/dbruı

instagram.com/dbruı

55046149R00082

Made in the USA
Middletown, DE
14 July 2019